# THE STRENGTH TO CARRY

AN ADVENT BIBLE STUDY ON MARY

# THE STRENGTH TO CARRY

FAITH FOR THE LIFE
YOU DIDN'T CHOOSE

LISA TONEY

Abingdon Women | Nashville

**The Strength to Carry**

Faith for the Life You Didn't Choose



ISBN 978-1-7910-4-5982



Cover description: Features a nighttime desert landscape beneath a star-filled sky, where a cloaked woman riding a donkey travels toward the distant lights of a town. A bright star shines overhead, illuminating the scene. The title, The Strength to Carry, appears in large gold and white letters near the top, with the subtitle, Faith for the Life You Didn't Choose, in smaller gold type below. A banner across the top identifies it as An Advent Bible Study on Mary. The author's name, Lisa Toney, appears in large gold letters at the bottom, alongside a badge indicating video and leader access is included.

MANUFACTURED IN THE UNITED STATES OF AMERICA

*For Zoe, Gus, Pax, and Eden,*
*who call me Mom.*
*You are the four lives*
*God placed in my arms and in my heart.*
*Watching you grow*
*has been one of the greatest joys of my life.*

*May you always remember*
*that the God who created you*
*will walk with you*
*and give you the strength*
*to carry whatever lies ahead.*

# Contents

# About the Author

Hello, I'm Lisa!

"For ***THIS*** we have Jesus!"

This is my battle cry! In every situation, it seems to apply. Jesus makes all the difference in the world!

Every morning, I am shocked, overjoyed, humbled, and bursting with gratitude for God's goodness. Out of this overflow, I love to speak and write about ways to build easy, intentional, and powerful faith habits to live for Jesus. As a professor and pastor, I love to help people answer the "why" behind the faith habits I teach.

I've listened, learned, taught, and served alongside the church for over twenty years. As the founder of Faith Habits, it is a joy to provide faith-based classes, coaching, and resources to encourage engagement with God.

With an MDiv from Fuller Theological Seminary and a communications degree from Taylor University, faith and communication are my passions. Partnering with Women of Faith, Aspire Women's Events, and Guideposts are some of the super fun opportunities God has brought my way.

I have authored the projects *Perfectly Flawed: God Transforms Our Weaknesses to Strengths*, *Not One Moment Late: Trusting God's Timing for Your Life*, *Thrive: Live Like You Matter*, *The Scripture Challenge*, and The Wholehearted Psalms Devotion series.

After growing up in the Midwest, I discovered I'm solar-powered and now live in Southern California with my husband, four kids, a puppy, a gecko, and four chickens. My husband and I often lead faith-based group tours of the Bible lands (Israel, Greece, Italy, Turkey, etc.) and walk where the unstoppable, incomparable, life-changing movement of Jesus began.

Let's be friends!

Instagram: LisaToneyLife
YouTube: Lisa Toney
Facebook: LisaToneyLife
www: lisatoney.com

# About This Study

Well, hey there, friend! I'm so glad that you picked up this Bible study.

Welcome to *The Strength to Carry: Faith for the Life You Didn't Choose!* If you are doing this during Advent and the Christmas season—*Merry Christmas!* This is going to be such a fun way to connect with Mary as we head toward that glorious birthday celebration of our King!

If you are doing this study during another time of the year, awesome sauce. We are going to dive into God's Word and study one of my favorite parts of the Bible: the arrival of Jesus, who is Emmanuel—God with us.

Over the next four weeks, we are going to walk closely with Mary and the people surrounding the birth of Jesus. Her story is one of the most beautiful and surprising stories in Scripture. But it's also a story filled with uncertainty, courage, and trust. Mary's life did not unfold the way she likely expected. She was a young woman living an ordinary life when God interrupted her plans with an extraordinary calling. The road that followed required courage, surrender, and deep faith.

And these are just a few reasons why her story matters so much to us today. Because many of us are also living lives we didn't fully choose. Maybe the path you are on includes unexpected responsibilities, disappointments, losses, or challenges you never imagined facing. Maybe your story includes detours that left you wondering where God is in the middle of it all.

Mary's story reminds us that God often does His most powerful work through lives that feel ordinary, interrupted, or even overwhelmed. Throughout this study, you will:

- **Discover how God meets us in unexpected seasons**. Mary's story shows us that God is present even when life takes a direction we didn't plan.
- **Learn how to trust God when the future feels uncertain.** Mary moved forward in obedience without knowing all the details. Her example helps us grow in courage when God calls us to trust Him.
- **See how God strengthens us to carry what He allows.** When life feels heavy, God does not leave us to carry it alone. His grace meets us in the middle of our calling, our struggles, and our waiting.

- **Experience the hope of Emmanuel, God with us.** The birth of Jesus is not just a beautiful Christmas story. It is the declaration that God stepped into our world and walks with us through every season.

As you spend time in Scripture each day, my prayer is that you will begin to see your own life through the lens of God's faithfulness. The same God who strengthened Mary is the same God who walks with you today.

And when the road feels unexpected or heavy, you will remember: God always provides the strength to carry what He places in our hands.

As you embrace this study, I encourage you to carve out some time each day, get out your Bible and a pen, and curl up in a cozy place to read through the passages and answer the questions. The goal is to get to know Mary and God more deeply. Allow Mary's story and the lessons from Scripture to enter your heart and mind. Let them shape your thinking, relationships, and choices. That is impact. That is long-lasting. That is transformation.

If you have some days when you are pressed for time, please feel free to condense your day to reading the Scripture passages. This will allow you to engage with Mary's story and stay active with your group. If there are questions you don't know how to answer, please feel free to skip them. The goal is to enjoy this time with the Lord, not get frustrated. So adapt it as you need.

If you're wondering if this study is right for you or if you're ready for it, know this: This study is for everyone, and your willingness demonstrates your readiness. Whether you are an experienced Bible study pro or just starting out, this study is meant to draw you closer to Jesus. There are many ways to seek Him, but a study allows you to gain new knowledge and wrestle with some deeper questions about life.

Personally, I have found that what I put into a Bible study is strongly connected to what I get out of that Bible study. When I can commit to daily time with Jesus, it changes my outlook on life. Mostly, it helps me start my day by getting my mindset right—I think a little more like Jesus and a little less like this world. Those daily study times allow me to saturate my struggles with Jesus rather than worry.

So setting your alarm clock thirty minutes earlier in the morning to get up and spend time with God might just reshape your whole outlook for the day, as well as your heart, leading you to live more like Jesus.

## FRIENDS MAKE EVERYTHING BETTER!

I've also found that I love doing a Bible study such as this one with friends. Whether you gather a group together in person or online, or you join a Bible study at church or work, it's always more fun with friends! Are there six to ten women you would love to hang out with for a few weeks? Maybe they are already your ride-or-dies. Maybe they are women you would like to get to know better.

I love being invited to things, don't you? Even if I can't go, I love being asked. It makes me feel valued and included. I bet if you text ten women, you'll probably end up with a group of six who are excited to join you! And just like that, you've got an amazing community with whom to share your life and talk about your faith for the next few weeks. Here's a sample text you can use.

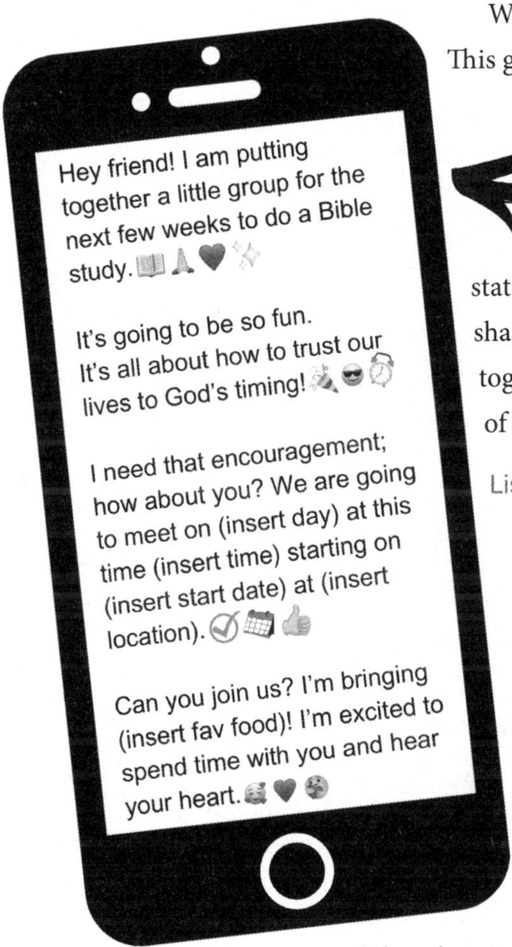


We need more friends in our lives. We need more of Jesus. This gives us the chance to do both!

According to a recent study by the Cigna Group, almost 60 percent of women say they're lonely.[1] That's six out of every ten women you know. Let's change that statistic and encourage women to connect with one another, share their lives, get intentional with Jesus, and pray together. We can change that statistic, and we'll have a lot of fun doing it!

List the people you would like to do this study with:

A group gathering for your Bible study is also a great way to stick with it and have a little life-giving accountability. Accountability with others helps prevent a fall into the unfinished Bible study abyss! (That abyss is lame. Don't go there.)

## WHAT EACH DAY LOOKS LIKE

Each week of this study includes five daily readings designed to help you slow down, open your Bible, and engage with God's Word in a meaningful way. Every day you will spend time reading Scripture, reflecting on what it means, and applying it to your life.

Here's what you can expect each day.

### A Focus Verse

We'll start each week with a power-packed, oh-so-helpful **focus verse** to get your mind on Jesus. You'll write it out and start to get it hardwired into your head and heart. You'll be amazed at how God wants to use this in your life! Each day before you begin your study time, here's how you can interact with your focus verse:

- read your focus verse;
- say your focus verse out loud;
- say the verse slowly and pause on phrases and words;
- highlight and circle words that stick out to you; and
- each day of your study, practice using the fill-in-the-blank space to write your focus verse out to learn it. Then live it.

### Scripture Exploration

You'll open your Bible and read passages connected to Mary's story and the coming of Jesus. Along the way, you'll answer questions that help you notice details, understand context, and reflect on what God may be saying to you.

### Reflection Questions

These questions are designed to help you process the passage personally. They invite you to consider how God's Word connects with your own experiences, struggles, and hopes.

### Take-Action Sections

Each week, you'll find a Take Action section that is filled with simple activities that invite you to step away from the page and interact with God through humor, His creation, a craft, or service project. These moments are meant to help you slow down and experience God's presence in everyday life.

### Worship

Each day, you'll see a QR code that will lead you to a worship song. This is a great way to spend time with God through music.

### Video Teaching

You can access the weekly video teaching on Amplify Media via the QR code on page 6.

You do not have to complete every section or question perfectly. This study is not about checking boxes; it is about encountering Jesus through His Word.

You get to decide how you want to interact with this material. Adulting has its perks. No one is going to force you into this. And above all, let me just say, you are invited. I invite you to rearrange your day to include this study.

If you don't have time, please talk to the person who manages your time and schedule immediately. Oh, wait, is that you?

With that said, sometimes we are just in a space where it is hard to add one more thing. I get it! Whether you are working a lot, have children, or are new to the faith (welcome, by the way—I'm so glad you are giving this a go), just picking up this book was a huge step for you. I got you. And, well done. I've been in all of those places, and choosing to be intentional about growing closer to Jesus amid busyness could just be the best thing for you. Let me be so bold as to say, it's a game changer.

I am learning more and more about trusting God to give me the strength to carry all that He has entrusted me with. Rarely does my life, or even my day, go as planned.

## SPECIAL NOTE FOR THOSE NEW TO BIBLE STUDY

This Bible study is structured so that you will look up many different verses in the Bible. In this way, you'll become more familiar with being in your Bible and start to see some of the connections in the full counsel of God's Word. Feel free to use the table of contents in your Bible to help you find the location of each book.

If a question is too hard or doesn't make sense to you, no problem; please feel free to skip it. My goal is to help you spend time with Jesus and learn to love both your Bible and Jesus! You get to choose your level of engagement. If you only have time (or patience) for a few questions each day, no worries. God can still use that!

## HOW TO USE THIS STUDY WITH A GROUP

This study is designed to be meaningful whether you do it on your own or with a group of friends. If you are doing this study on your own, don't worry, you are still part of a larger community of women who are walking through these same pages and learning the same truths.

You might consider inviting a friend to join you. Because faith grows stronger when we walk together. There is something special about learning and growing together. If you are doing this study with others, I encourage you to meet once a week to watch the teaching video and discuss what you have been learning. These conversations often become the places where God's truth sinks even deeper into our hearts.

Your group gatherings can be simple. You might:

- watch the weekly teaching video together,
- share one thing God showed you during the week,
- discuss the provided questions, or
- pray for one another.

Some groups meet in living rooms with coffee, tea, and snacks. Others gather online or meet at church. There is no perfect formula; what matters most is creating space to encourage one another in faith.

The video teachings also include an optional, introductory teaching so that you can gather your group for a kickoff session to meet everyone in your group, watch the introduction video, and get excited about this study together—a format that would make this a five-week study. You can choose which works best for you and your group.

As we journey together, we will prayerfully ask the Holy Spirit to show up in mighty ways and transform our lives daily. Here is your opportunity to think through what time will be best for you to work on your daily homework.

I plan to do my study at this time ______________ a.m./p.m. on these days:

____ M ____ T ____ W ____ Th ____ F ____ Sat ____ Sun

at this location ______________________________.

Write a prayer of expectation and anticipation to Jesus here:

## AN INVITATION TO TRUST GOD

God often meets us in the places we never planned to go. The life we imagined may look different from the life we are living, and the road ahead may feel heavier than we expected. Yet Scripture reminds us that God does not abandon us in those moments. Instead, He walks beside us, strengthening our hearts and steadying our steps. When the burdens feel overwhelming, His grace becomes sufficient. When the path feels uncertain, His presence becomes our guide. The same God who strengthened Mary to carry the calling placed before her promises to strengthen us as well. What feels impossible in our own strength becomes possible when we trust the One who walks with us. And over time, what once felt like a burden we could never bear becomes a testimony of God's faithfulness. Trusting Him transforms unexpected roads into sacred ones, weakness into dependence, and heavy burdens into opportunities to experience the strength to carry.

When the road is harder than expected.

When the burden feels heavier than planned.

Remember that God always gives us . . .

THE
STRENGTH
TO CARRY

**Looking for additional promotional and study resources for this study?**

**Visit lisatoney.com/ thestrengthtocarryresources**

# VIDEO VIEWER GUIDE: INTRODUCTION

The wonder of Christmas was meant to be ____________.

But the Christmas story was never meant to feel __________.

Advent is a season of waiting and ____________________.

The God who writes our story is also the God who gives us the _____________ to carry it.

# DISCUSSION QUESTIONS: INTRODUCTION

Let's get to know one another!

- Share your name and the people and the animals you live with.

- Where do you spend your time most days of the week?

- What is one of your favorite things about Christmas?

- What do you like to do for fun?

- Share your "why" for being part of this study. What are you hoping the Lord will do through this in your life?

Write down the names of the people in your small group. You have a great opportunity for the next four weeks to get to know, encourage, pray with, and build friendships with them. We all need people around us to help us carry what God has invited us into!

# WEEK 1

# STARTLED

## The Path You Didn't Choose

### FOCUS VERSE

*"For no word from God will ever fail."*
*Luke 1:37*

# Take Action

## A Little Mary-ment

What did Adam say the day before Christmas?

It's Christmas Eve!

HA HA HA

LOL

## SERVE

Pack some boxes for Operation Christmas Child with Samaritan's Purse.

# Startled

## Creation Corner

Take a slow walk and look closely at the ground instead of the horizon. Notice tiny details—an ant trail, moss on a rock, a small flower growing through a crack in the sidewalk. Sometimes the most extraordinary things are hidden in ordinary places. Where might God be working in quiet or unnoticed ways in your life right now?

Read Luke 1:48

## CREATE

Cut out a variety of snowflakes from white cardstock or paper and hang them with fishline from the ceiling for an indoor winter wonderland.

# Moments with Mary

*But Mary treasured up all these things and pondered them in her heart.*
*Luke 2:19*

The evening air in Nazareth carried the smell of warm wheat bread and crushed olives. I had just finished grinding grain beside my mother and sweeping the packed dirt floor of our small home. Outside, children's laughter drifted through the narrow streets while the voices of women greeting one another in the streets could be heard.

Life here is quiet and predictable. Every girl expects the same path—marriage, children, and faithfulness to the God of our fathers and mothers. Joseph and I are betrothed. Soon, he was to bring me to the home he is preparing for us. Or so I thought.

Tonight I was praying beside the small oil lamp in the corner of our house when the room suddenly filled with light. My heart raced as a messenger of the Lord, a real angel, stood before me. He was magnificent. He was strong, powerful, full of light, and radiating the glory of heaven.

I was afraid at first, but the angel, named Gabriel, told me not to be afraid because God had found favor with me. Favor? How could I be favored by God? I'm not anyone important. God knew me? Here in our little village of Nazareth?

I can barely find the words to explain what happened. Gabriel said that I was to conceive and give birth to a son. My mind struggled to understand. I was a virgin and had not yet been with Joseph. Yet the angel said the Holy

Spirit would overshadow me and that this miraculous child would be called the Son of the Most High. A life placed inside me by God Himself. Could this really be? The Messiah? The Promised One our people have been waiting for? The One who will right all wrongs and bring us freedom? I was overjoyed and terrified. Why me? What will people say? What will Joseph think when he hears that I am with child?

My heart trembled between fear and faith. The angel left, but God's peace remained with me. The words of the prophet steadied my spirit.

> "For my thoughts are not your thoughts,
> neither are your ways My ways,"
> declares the LORD.
>
> Isaiah 55:8

I did not choose this path. But if the Lord has chosen me to carry His promise, then He will give me the strength to carry what comes with it. So tonight I whispered the only words I could say:

"I am the Lord's servant. . . .
May your word to me be fulfilled."

Mary

# DAY 1: JUST ANOTHER TUESDAY UNTIL GOD SHOWS UP

**Focus Verse**

*"For no word from God will ever fail."*

*Luke 1:37*

I'm a troll. Legitimately. I grew up under the bridge. If you're from Michigan, you get it. Michigan has two peninsulas and one bridge that connects them. If you grew up on the lower peninsula *under* the Mackinac Bridge, you're a "troll." If you grew up *above* it, you're a "yooper." Two peninsulas. One bridge. And a whole lot of opinions about which one is better.

I grew up in a small town in the northern part of the lower peninsula of Michigan. And if you've ever lived in a small town, you know this: It's hard to hide. Everyone knows everyone. They know your family. They know your story. They know your business—sometimes before you do. It's a gift, and sometimes, it's a challenge. My town is so small it's technically a village.

I want to invite you to step into another small village. Nazareth. Nazareth is in the northern region of Israel. It wasn't fancy. It wasn't famous. It had anywhere from two hundred to five hundred people. Later in Scripture, someone would ask: "Can anything good come out of Nazareth?" (John 1:46).[1] It didn't have a great reputation.[2] But God chose this town from which to reach down from heaven and invite a young woman to join Him in changing the world.

She didn't ask for it. She didn't plan for it. She didn't see it coming. One of the most well-known women in history, Mary, was from this tiny, relatively unknown village, Nazareth.

Mary was likely a young teenage girl, who was twelve to fifteen years old,[3] living in a tight-knit community where life followed familiar rhythms. She helped to care for her family. She was gaining the skills she would need to manage her own household one day. Drawing water. Preparing food. Gardening. Running errands. Walking the same roads day after day.

As a betrothed woman, she was not yet married, but committed to her future husband, Joseph. In the first century, betrothal was just as binding as marriage.[4] Mary likely spent her days daydreaming about her future with Joe. Would they have children soon? What would their life together become?

She was both excited and a little nervous. This was the natural next step. Expected. Honored. Ordinary.

As a young Jewish woman, Mary knew the Scriptures. She had grown up hearing the stories. She had learned the promises. She worshipped in the synagogue with her family. She had celebrated the festivals at the Temple. She loved God deeply. She was proud of her people and their history.

God chose Nazareth. God chose a small and ordinary place. And God chose Mary.

Mary didn't look like a headline. She looked like everyone else. She had a routine. A future she thought she understood. A life that made sense. Nothing about her day would have made anyone stop and say, "*That's the one. That's the girl God is about to use to change the world.*"

But God saw Mary, in a way that only He can. He wasn't looking for impressive. He wasn't looking for a platform. He wasn't looking for perfect circumstances. He was looking for a heart that was ready. And maybe just maybe He still is.

Where in your life feels ordinary right now?

How do you think God prepares people in the middle of the ordinary?

Read Luke 1:26-27 and Matthew 1:18. What do you learn about Mary?

## FAITH HABIT

Make your bed and dedicate your day to God out loud.

God is not looking for impressive. Read 1 Samuel 16:7. What does God look at when He chooses someone?

God is looking for a willing person. Mary's life began with faithfulness, a life positioned in such a way that when God spoke, she was ready to listen.

We often underestimate the power of ordinary seasons. But it is exactly where God shapes and prepares us. Because when God chooses someone for something significant, He often finds them in the middle of an ordinary day. God does some of His most powerful work in places the world overlooks. God is looking for hearts that are available, not impressive.

Then everything changed. Then heaven stepped into her ordinary life. A messenger from God would stand in front of her. Nothing would ever be the same.

**God is looking for hearts that are available, not impressive.**

> CARRY THIS WITH YOU
> *Ordinary You. Extraordinary God.*

**Get your worship on with Elevation Worship and sing "Available."**

## LEARN IT. LIVE IT.

Try filling in the blanks of this week's focus verse. You can go back and look if you need to! Each day give it a go and see if you have it down by the end of the week.

*"For no _______ from _____ will ever _______."*

*Luke 1:37*

# DAY 2: WHEN GOD MESSES WITH YOUR PLANS

**Focus Verse**

*"For no word from God will ever fail."*

*Luke 1:37*

I was driving home when my phone rang. I didn't answer it because I didn't recognize the number. It was just another phone call that I figured was spam. I was driving home from work like I do most days. Same old, same old. But then the same number called again. And for some reason I decided to answer it.

On the other end was unexpected news. My daughter had just been awarded a scholarship she had already been told she didn't get. We had received the "no" email. We had processed the disappointment. We had moved on. We had already started figuring out what Plan B could look like.

And then the phone rang.

Everything changed.

What we thought was settled wasn't settled. What we thought was over wasn't over. We thought the answer was no, but God wasn't finished yet.

Some interruptions feel inconvenient. Some feel frustrating. But some are invitations. Moments when God steps into what we thought we understood and rewrites the story.

That's exactly where Mary found herself. One ordinary day. One unexpected moment. And everything was about to change. Suddenly, the ordinary space she stood in was no longer ordinary. The room was filled with light. The atmosphere shifted. Heaven broke in.

An angel, Gabriel, a messenger who stood in the presence of God, appeared before her.[5] And the message he carried would change everything.

Read Luke 1:26-37. What does Gabriel say to Mary?

What is her initial response?

What does the angel tell her not to be afraid of?

What impossible thing does the angel say will happen?

**Mary was simply living her life. And then God interrupted.**

Mary wasn't looking for this moment. She wasn't asking for a sign. She wasn't trying to stand out. She was simply living her life. And then God interrupted.

Have you ever experienced an interruption that changed everything? Not something you planned. Not something you would have chosen. But something that shifted your direction?

Where in your life have you experienced an unexpected interruption?

What if that interruption wasn't random? What if it was an invitation? What if God was in it? Is there a situation in your life right now that feels unexpected, inconvenient, or unclear?

God often speaks in interruptions. Look up Proverbs 16:9. Where have your plans shifted but God still showed up?

### FAITH HABIT: PAUSE BEFORE YOU REACT

Today, when something interrupts your plans, ask, "God, could You be in this?"

We like plans. We like clarity. We like knowing what comes next. But God doesn't always work within the structure we create. Sometimes He breaks in.

Right in the middle of what we thought we understood. Mary's life made sense until it didn't.

And when God spoke, it didn't make her life easier. It made it different. More complicated. More costly. More significant. Because when God interrupts, it's not to disrupt your life. He is inviting you into something greater.

Look up Isaiah 55:8-9. How does this verse help explain why God's interruptions feel confusing?

Interruptions are not random, but divine redirection. The angel's message to Mary included something that didn't seem possible. But the angel makes her a promise. Remember our focus verse: "For no word from God will ever fail" (Luke 1:37).

God's Word is not limited by the things that we obsess over. Like our timelines. Or our bank accounts. Or our job titles. Or our failures. Even when life shifts unexpectedly, God is still at work.

**Worship and sing "Mary Did You Know?" by Tommee Profitt featuring Jordan Smith.**

**CARRY THIS WITH YOU**
*Didn't See It Coming. God Did.*

### LEARN IT. LIVE IT.

Fill in the blanks of this week's focus verse.

*"For no _______ from _____ will ever _______."*
*Luke 1:37*

# DAY 3: THE KIND OF "YES" THAT CHANGES EVERYTHING

**Focus Verse**

> *"For no word from God will ever fail."*
>
> *Luke 1:37*

I have three, almost four, teenagers in my house. And I love them dearly. I really do. But I don't know what happened. Somewhere along the way, their language skills seem to have regressed. I get more grunts, head nods, and eye rolls than should be legal. I'm constantly trying to get actual words out of them.

"How was your day?" "Good."

"What did you do?" "Nothing."

"How are you feeling?" "Fine."

But the one that makes me go completely cross-eyed, cuckoo bananas is "yep." I don't know why it bothers me so much, but it does. All I want is a full, complete, intentional "yes." Not a shrug. Not a half-response. Not something mumbled while walking away. A real "yes."

Because there's a difference, isn't there? Between a casual response and a committed one. Between mumbling and meaning it.

Jesus said it this way: "All you need to say is simply 'Yes' or 'No'" (Matthew 5:37). In other words, be clear, be honest, be wholehearted. Say what you mean. And mean what you say.

And that's exactly the moment Mary finds herself in. God has spoken. The invitation has been given. And now she has a choice. Not just to respond, but to respond fully. Not halfway. Not casually. But with a whole, surrendered yes.

Read Luke 1:34-38. What question does Mary ask before she responds?

What does the angel say about how this will happen?

Who is the example that the angel gives to build her faith?

What is Mary's final response to God?

Mary had questions. She didn't fully understand. She didn't have all the details. And yet she still said yes. Not because it was easy. But because she trusted God.

Have you ever felt God nudging you toward something that didn't fully make sense yet? Something that required trust before clarity? Where might God be inviting you to say yes right now?

What is holding you back from saying yes? Fear? Uncertainty? Control? Comfort?

FAITH HABIT

Say yes to one thing you've been avoiding that you know is right.

**God's invitations often require surrender before they make sense.**

Mary's yes wasn't casual.[6] It was obedience—with a side of courage. She was saying yes to something that would change her life. All her plans, her reputation, and her future would look different. This wasn't a safe yes. It was a surrendered one.

A lot of us want to say yes to God as long as we understand everything first. As long as it fits our timeline. As long as it feels comfortable. But that's not how God works.

God's invitations often require surrender before they make sense. Mary didn't say, "Let me think about it." Or, "Um . . . can I get back to you?" Or, "Can you give me more details?"

None of that. Instead, she said: "I am the Lord's servant. May your word to me be fulfilled" (Luke 1:38).

*That* is a full yes.

Look up these verses about responding to God with obedience. As you read, notice what each one reveals about saying yes to Him.

- James 1:22
- Luke 11:28
- Hebrews 11:8
- John 14:15
- 1 Samuel 15:22
- Deuteronomy 5:33

Which one speaks most powerfully to you today? Why? What would it look like to live this verse out today?

Mary's yes didn't just affect her. It changed the world. Your yes to God is never just about you; it creates space for God to move in ways you cannot yet see.

And the promise still stands: “For no word from God will ever fail” (Luke 1:37).

If God is asking, He is able.

If God is calling, He is faithful.

If God is leading, you can trust Him.

**CARRY THIS WITH YOU**

*Surrender First. Understand Later.*

Enjoy a time of worship with “Be Born in Me” by Francesca Battistelli.

## LEARN IT. LIVE IT.

Fill in the blanks of this week’s focus verse.

*“For no _______ from _____ will ever _______.”*

*Luke 1:37*

# DAY 4: STOP SPIRALING. START HOLDING.

**Focus Verse**

*"For no word from God will ever fail."*
*Luke 1:37*

Some nights I lie awake. I'm tired. I'm ready for bed. I'm ready for sleep. But my brain? Absolutely not. It's like my body clocks out and my mind clocks in for the night shift. And suddenly, I'm replaying a conversation from earlier in the day. *Why did I say that? Why did I say it like that? Why didn't I say something different?*

And then I start editing the conversation. "Oh, I should've said this." "No, wait, this would've been better." Like a never-ending Groundhog Day moment I didn't sign up for. Five times. Ten times. Why are we still here? Still awkward. Still me. It's ridiculous. It's irrational. I can't change it. But my brain is like, "Let's run it again just in case."

After Mary said yes to this huge life-changing moment, she could put her hand on her stomach and know that there was a baby growing in there who was miraculous. How in the world was she going to explain this to her parents? And to Joseph? And to *everyone*?

But what Mary did next was very different. She didn't spiral. She didn't try to control the moment. She responded in a way that is easy for us to read right over. Later in her story, we get a glimpse into how she carried everything God was doing in her life.

Let's skip ahead just a bit and take a look at this one sentence describing Mary's reaction to the events surrounding giving birth to the baby Jesus.

Read Luke 2:19. What does Mary do with everything she has experienced?

Now go back and read Luke 1:34-38. What has Mary just said yes to?

### FAITH HABIT: HOLD IT DIFFERENTLY

Write what's bothering you, then write: "God is here."

Mary didn't rush past the moment. She didn't ignore what she was feeling. She didn't try to solve it. She held it.

Have you ever found yourself replaying something over and over again? Trying to fix it, figure it out, or control the outcome? What is something your mind keeps returning to right now?

There is a difference between replaying and holding something with intention. One leads you deeper into anxiety. The other leads you deeper into trust. We tend to replay what we cannot control. We go over it again and again, hoping clarity will come or something will change.

But Mary shows us another way. She held with care what God had done and what the angel had said. She didn't rush it. She didn't try to force understanding. She let it settle. She returned to what was true instead of getting lost in what she didn't understand.

Perhaps Mary held onto Psalm 119:11: "I have hidden your word in my heart."

And Psalm 62:5: "Yes, my soul, find rest in God."

Before Mary could live this story in front of others, she had to let it settle deeply within herself. Luke 2:19 gives us a bit of a glimpse into how Mary navigated this adventure with God. She soaked it all in and was at peace. She had the kind of peace of God that "surpasses all understanding" (Philippians 4:7 ESV). She chose to hold onto what God had said more than what she felt.

**There is a difference between replaying and holding something with intention. One leads you deeper into anxiety. The other leads you deeper into trust.**

Get your worship on and sing "Breath of Heaven (Mary's Song)" by Amy Grant.

Because the promise still stood: "For no word from God will ever fail" (Luke 1:37).

Even in the quiet. Even in the waiting. Even when our thoughts won't slow down. God is still at work.

CARRY THIS WITH YOU

*Hold the Word. Drop the Worry.*

## LEARN IT. LIVE IT.

Fill in the blanks of this week's focus verse.

*"For no _______ from _____ will ever _______."*

*Luke 1:37*

# DAY 5: THAT-A-GIRL. WALK. IT. OUT.

**Focus Verse**

*"For no word from God will ever fail."*
Luke 1:37

Ice cream walks after dinner are just the best. When school gets out, this becomes a nightly rhythm. The kids grab ice cream. I grab the dog (who thinks every walk is the greatest day of her life), and we head out around the neighborhood. Now this is not one of my power walks. There is no speed. There is no sweating. There is definitely no "closing my rings." This is more like a stroll. We talk about everything, laugh at the dog, chat with the neighbors, and we celebrate that summer has officially arrived.

When we go to Michigan for a visit with my family, our walks level up. My sisters, my mom, all of the family dogs, and some of our what feels like *all forty-seven children* (it's actually twelve, but it feels like more) go walking together. And this walk? It's up a hill. A real hill. The kind where you're halfway up thinking, *"Will we make it? Will my dog make it?"* But somehow we're talking, laughing, catching up, and before you know it, we've made it to the top. That's the beauty of walking with people. You don't just get somewhere. You connect while you're moving.

Following God looks a lot more like a walk than a plan. Mary didn't just have a moment with God. She got up and she walked it out.

**Following God looks a lot more like a walk than a plan.**

Read Luke 1:39-40. What does Mary do next?

Mary didn't stay where she was. She moved.

Have you ever noticed how easy it is to feel stuck, even after you know what God is asking? We think about it. We pray about it. We process it. But we don't always move.

Where in your life do you feel like you're standing still right now?

What is one step you know God is inviting you to take?

Obedience to God is not just something we feel. It's something we walk out. Scripture says Mary left Nazareth and made the journey to her relative Elizabeth's house in the Judean Hill Country.

She didn't delay. She didn't overthink it. She didn't wait until everything made sense. She moved. God didn't give her the full roadmap. But he did give her a direction. The angel told Mary that Elizabeth was receiving a miracle too. So in the midst of all the questions and potential awkward conversations to be had, God gave Mary the gift of some time to process and someone to process with.

Her rocky road trip from Nazareth to southern Judea was about one hundred miles.[7] If she walked twenty miles a day, she was looking at about a journey of four to five days. Close to a week of walking and talking with the Lord. Praying. Feeling all the feels. Excited. Scared. Hopeful. Doubtful. Determined.

That-a-girl. Walk. It. Out.

Walk. Think. Pray.

Walk. Think. Pray.

Repeat all day, every day.

Good plan.

Have you ever needed some alone time to process something big before sharing it? What was the occasion? Why was that alone time important? How did God use it to accomplish His good purpose in you?

## FAITH HABIT: WALK IT OUT

Take a walk and talk to God about the next steps in your life.

Look up these verses that talk about walking with God. Circle your favorite.

- Leviticus 26:12
- Deuteronomy 5:33
- Psalm 23:4
- Micah 6:8

Write out the one that you feel God is most speaking into your life today. How does it connect to your life?

Read Romans 8:28. When does God work His good?

Read Philippians 2:12-13. Who is working in your life to bring about His good?

**Get your worship on and sing: "Trust in God" by Elevation Worship.**

God was working His good plans in Mary's life. God was actually working out good for everyone's life in this unexpected pregnancy, but that must have been way hard to see. God's work is sometimes hard to understand. We want the whole plan. God often gives only the next step.

Walking with God means continuing forward, even when you cannot see very far ahead. It's about staying close enough to God to keep moving when He leads. Mary didn't know how her story would unfold. But she trusted the One who was writing it. So she got up and she walked.

Galatians 5:25 describes walking with God in this way: "If we live by the Spirit, let us also keep in step with the Spirit."

What does it look like to "keep in step" with God in your everyday life?

**CARRY THIS WITH YOU**
*Keep Walking. God's Working.*

## LEARN IT. LIVE IT.

Fill in the blanks of this week's focus verse.

*"For no _______ from _____ will ever _______."*

*Luke 1:37*

# VIDEO VIEWER GUIDE: WEEK 1

Interruptions are often ____________________.

___________ begins where control ends.

Life is where our faith grows ______________ than our fear.

Faith does not require perfect ____________.

The place that startles us the most . . . is the very place where God is

____________ at work.

# DISCUSSION QUESTIONS: WEEK 1

- What's a small moment in your life that suddenly took an unexpected turn like Lisa's sesame seed story?
- When you picture Mary living her ordinary life in Nazareth before the angel appeared, what stands out to you about the way God chose to begin this story?
- Can you think of a time when your plans were suddenly interrupted or redirected? What emotions did you feel in that moment?
- Lisa said, "Interruptions are often invitations." What do you think God might invite us to in seasons when life doesn't go according to plan?
- Mary responded to the angel by saying, "I am the Lord's servant." What do you think helped her trust God enough to say yes in such an uncertain moment?
- What do you need to trust God with this week?

# Week 2

# STRENGTHENED

## Believing Big Promises

## FOCUS VERSE

*Blessed is she who has believed that the Lord would fulfill his promises to her!*
Luke 1:45

# Take Action

## A Little Mary-ment

Why were the wise men such good gift givers?

Because they understood the value of presence.

HA HA HA

LoL

## SERVE

Participate or host an Angel Tree to provide gifts for kids whose parents are in jail.

PRISON FELLOWSHIP ANGEL TREE

# Strengthened

## Creation Corner

Step outside and look at the sky for a few minutes. Notice the clouds, the color, and the movement of the air. Mary spent much of her life outdoors. The same sky you see today is the sky she would have seen in Nazareth. The God who placed the stars also placed His calling on Mary's life—and on yours. What does it remind you of to know the Creator of the universe knows your name?

Read Psalm 147:4–5

## CREATE

Create a vintage ornament wreath. Start with a tinsel wreath and trim down the pine needles. Hot glue on vintage ornament bulbs tightly next to one another so that the whole wreath is a shiny statement piece!

# Moments with Mary

*But Mary treasured up all these things and pondered them in her heart.*
*Luke 2:19*

The road from Nazareth to the hill country of Judea was long and dusty. For almost a week, for protection from robbers, I traveled south with a small group making the same journey. Our path wound through rocky hills and quiet valleys where shepherds watched their flocks. At night, we rested near small fires, sharing bread, dried figs, and stories from the road.

With every step, I carried the quiet miracle growing inside me. The angel had told me that my relative Elizabeth was also expecting a child. Elizabeth, who had waited her whole life with empty arms, whispered prayers to the Lord, begging for the gift of a child. If anyone could understand what God was doing in me, I thought perhaps it would be her.

By the time I reached Elizabeth's home, the sun was low and golden. Olive trees covered the slopes, their silver and green leaves moving gently in the evening wind. I approached Elizabeth's house with a racing heart. "Shalom," I called as I stepped inside. The moment Elizabeth heard my voice, she gasped and placed her hands on her stomach.

"Blessed are you among women, and blessed is the child you will bear!" I stood there in amazement. I had not told her anything. Yet somehow, she knew. Elizabeth came quickly and wrapped her arms around me with joy. Her laughter filled the house, and the fear that had quietly followed me since the angel came began to loosen its grip on my heart.

For the first time, I felt the deep comfort of being understood. That evening, we worked together in the courtyard milling flour, kneading dough, and placing bread into the clay oven. The smell of baking barley filled the air while the hills around us slowly darkened beneath the evening sky.

As the stars appeared, praise rose in my heart like a song.

"My soul glorifies the Lord
    and my spirit rejoices in God my Savior" (Luke 1:46).

God was doing something far greater than I could understand. I do not know what the days ahead will bring. There will surely be questions, whispers, and difficult moments. Yet tonight, resting in Elizabeth's home, I felt something steady growing alongside my fear.

Trust.

The God who began this work will give me the strength to carry it.

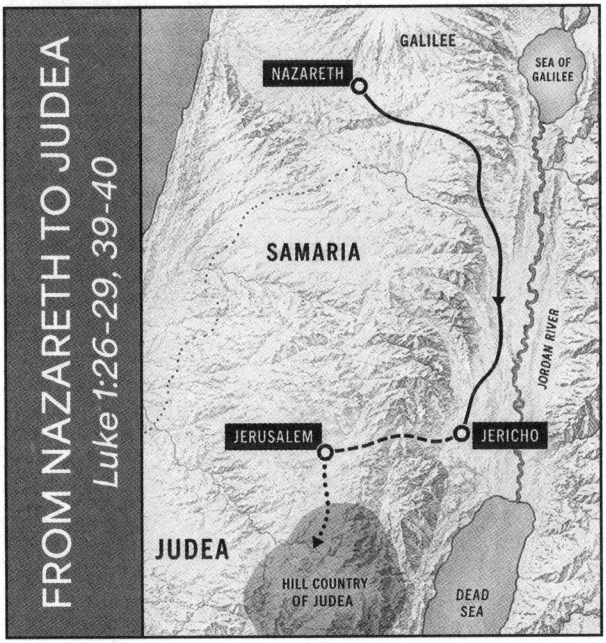


Mary

# DAY 1: GOD SAW YOU BEFORE YOU SAW IT

**Focus Verse**

*"Blessed is she who has believed that the Lord would fulfill his promises to her!"*

*Luke 1:45*

When I first moved to Pasadena, California, I didn't know anyone. Technically, I had a distant cousin who lived in Newport Beach. My mom kept encouraging me to reach out to her, but I was so busy with seminary and life that I never did. I kept thinking, *I'll get to it.*

But I didn't.

By the time I was finally ready to reach out she had moved away. Opportunity missed. I remember feeling so disappointed. Sometimes just knowing someone is nearby can make all the difference.

Part of Mary's story is a peek behind the curtain of what God was up to in the life of someone else. A relative. A woman named Elizabeth. Before Mary ever hears from an angel, God is already writing the story. And maybe that's true for you too. God may be honoring faithfulness that no one else notices.

About one hundred miles away from where Mary lived in Nazareth, in the Judean Hill Country near Jerusalem, God was already at work. A couple who qualified for all the senior discount deals was about to get the surprise of their lives.

Read Luke 1:5-7 to meet Liz and Zech (Elizabeth and Zechariah). Let's get into their story and learn a little more about them.

Who was the king at the time?

What was Zechariah's job?

What do we learn about Elizabeth's family line?

**FAITH HABIT**

Start your day by saying, "God, I give You today."

Can you feel their heartache after a lifetime of not being able to have a child? It's so hard. When we eagerly await something that does not come to pass, it can really shape us. Have you ever experienced that kind of disappointment? The kind where you prayed, you hoped, and you believed, and things still didn't turn out the way you wanted? Take a moment to be honest before God.

What is something in your life that has not gone the way you hoped?

**We all carry places in our lives that didn't unfold the way we imagined.**

I may not know exactly your situation, but we all carry places in our lives that didn't unfold the way we imagined. We all struggle with disappointment, loss of dreams, unexpected challenges, and parts of our lives that we wish were different. This is why this story is so epic. It changes everything.

Well, you are not going to believe this, but things were about to dramatically change for this couple. But before the breakthrough came, there were years of quiet faithfulness.

## THE BACKSTORY

Liz was like a pastor's wife. Zechariah was her hunka hunka *burnin' love* (stay with me!), who was also a priest for the nation of Israel. They'd celebrated a lot of anniversaries together: bronze, silver, and gold. They were heading into their golden years, together. They didn't have much, but they had each other. For years, they had prayed for a child, but God had not granted their prayers. It was hard. Liz and Zech waited and waited. As the years went by, they released the pain that came with their broken hearts. They trusted God in all things, even with their hurt and disappointment.

Trust. What a word. They would trust their God over their circumstances. Perhaps God intended for their home to be different from those of all their friends and family. Everyone they knew had families. All of Liz's friends sneezed and got pregnant. At least it felt that way. Liz wanted to stay strong, but she *still* did think about it every now and again, what with all her friends now having grandbabies and great-grandbabies. *Sigh.*

Trust. What a word. Liz would trust God over her circumstances. Zechariah and Elizabeth felt like they would be the last of their family tree, but God would endure forever. That was the most important thing.

And then things got interesting. Zech went into work one day, just like every day for decades. His Temple job required him to *burn* incense (*Liz's hunka burnin' love . . . get it?*) to God to display the love and obedience of his people. Zech had done this a hundred times, but it was *always* a weighty responsibility to represent the Israelites. His priestly order of the Levites was set apart from the other tribes. His heritage was a special calling. Even his name, Zechariah, meant "the Lord remembers." It was his duty, his honor, to help his people remember the faithfulness of God through his work at the Temple.

Zechariah didn't just randomly end up in the Temple that day. The priests served on a rotating schedule that had been established generations earlier. Each family line was assigned specific times to minister before the Lord. Zechariah belonged to the division of Abijah. If you're curious, read 1 Chronicles 24:1-19 to see how these priestly divisions were established. You can find his division specifically mentioned!

Zechariah and Elizabeth's story reveals something we often overlook because it feels boring. But God sees it as beautiful. Faithfulness. Long before the miracle. Long before anything visibly changes. They were faithful to God. Luke describes them as "righteous" (Luke 1:6). Righteous is a word that means "in right relationship."[1] By being faithful to God and trusting Him, they were in a right relationship with God and each other.

Day after day, Zechariah showed up. He went to the Temple. He did the work. He carried the responsibility he had been given. Nothing about that day felt extraordinary. And yet it mattered. Because God often does His greatest work in the places that feel the most ordinary.

In the showing up.

In the quiet obedience.

In the faithfulness that no one else sees.

If you are in a season where nothing feels like it's changing, where your prayers feel unanswered or your life doesn't look the way you hoped, God sees you. He really does. Your faithfulness is not wasted. It may be the very place where He is preparing something you cannot yet see.

**Our timing is not God's timing.**

God had been faithfully preparing something remarkable. Our timing is not God's timing. Showing up faithfully to what God has entrusted to us every day matters. God sees it. And God is sometimes working through it in ways we don't even know.

God is faithful to provide, sustain, and fulfill His promises—even when life doesn't look the way we expected. God provides what you need and is faithful to fulfill His promises. Look up these verses and discover what some of God's promises are to you.

- 2 Corinthians 9:8
- Philippians 4:19
- Jeremiah 29:11
- Proverbs 23:18
- Psalm 62:5

Every one of these verses points to the same truth: God provides what we need, holds our future, and never fails to keep His promises.

Write out which of these verses you most need to hold on to in this season. How is God speaking to you through it?

Enjoy this beautiful worship song and video: "Mother to a Savior and King" by Fiona Palomo.

**CARRY THIS WITH YOU**

*God's Already There.*

## LEARN IT. LIVE IT.

As we end our day, let's practice your focus verse. Try to fill in the blanks.

*"__________ is she who has __________ that the Lord would fulfill his __________ to her!"*

*Luke 1:45*

# DAY 2: WHILE YOU WERE WAITING, GOD WAS WORKING

**Focus Verse**

*"Blessed is she who has believed that the Lord would fulfill his promises to her!"*
*Luke 1:45*

I'd had a hard day at work. Some meetings had been really complicated. Emotions ran high. I love my work, but working with people is always an adventure. We are all imperfect, messy, and broken. Sometimes our rough edges show up and wound others. I was trying to help resolve some conflict and do mediation, and I was emotionally exhausted. I was driving home and talking to the Lord about it. I said, "Lord, I've been serving the church for a lot of years now."

God doesn't always respond to me like this, but in that moment I heard Him say, "I've been at it even longer than you." I just cracked up. True that, God. True that. It just shifted my perspective in an unexpected way. It gave me what I needed to keep going. Sometimes God shows up in the very ordinary moments of life—like driving home from work.

**Sometimes God shows up in the very ordinary moments of life.**

While Mary was living her ordinary life in Nazareth, God was already at work somewhere else. Quietly. Intentionally. Personally. About one hundred miles away, in the hill country of Judea, there was a woman named Elizabeth. And her story had been unfolding for years.

Read Luke 1:5-7. What do we learn about Elizabeth?

We don't know exactly how old Elizabeth was, but she was past childbearing age.[2] So likely she was in her fifties or sixties. God chose someone who could not get pregnant to reveal another miracle that would be connected to Mary and her miracle.

Read Luke 1:11-25. What happens when the angel appears to Zechariah?

What promise is given?

When Mary arrived at Elizabeth's house weary from a long trip, Elizabeth greets her with great joy. The baby in Elizabeth's womb was six months old and leaped in greeting when Mary and the baby in her womb approached. This baby was given to Elizabeth to be a relative of Jesus and prepare the way for Jesus. He would become John the Baptist.

John the Baptist was chosen by God to go ahead of Jesus and get people ready—to wake them up spiritually and call them back to God. John lived a bold and set-apart life in the wilderness, preaching repentance and inviting people to turn away from sin and return to the Lord. His message was clear and urgent: *Get ready. The Savior is coming.*

John's role was not to draw attention to himself, but to point people to Jesus. When Jesus began His ministry, John recognized Him immediately and declared, "Look, the Lamb of God, who takes away the sin of the world!" (John 1:29). He baptized Jesus in the Jordan River, marking the beginning of Jesus's public ministry. John understood his purpose with incredible humility, saying, "He must become greater; I must become less" (John 3:30). His life reminds us that sometimes God calls us to prepare the way for what He is doing, not to be the center of the story, but to faithfully point others to the One who is.

Elizabeth had no idea of the plans that God had for her baby, but she knew that he was special. God had given her a son, and God had given Mary a miracle baby. What is so cool is how Elizabeth greets Mary not with questions and doubt, but with faith.

Before Mary explains anything to her, she already knows. The Holy Spirit has been at work with revelations for Elizabeth to get her ready to greet Mary.

*"Blessed are you among women . . ."*

*"Blessed is the child you will bear . . ."*

*"The mother of my Lord . . ."*

Elizabeth calls the baby in Mary's womb her Lord. She knows that God has given Mary the promised Messiah for their people. This is one of the first human declarations of who Jesus was to be.

Elizabeth honors the miracle in Mary. She believes it by faith. That had to be so encouraging to Mary as she worried what everyone would say.

Elizabeth's story reminds us that silence does not mean God has stopped working. Even when nothing seems to be changing. Even when the answer hasn't come yet.

Where have you felt like God has been silent in your life?

What might it look like to trust that He is still working even now?

God's silence is not His absence; it is often His preparation. What feels like a delay to you may actually be God developing something deeper than you can see.

Preparing the moment.
Preparing the people.
Preparing you.

## FAITH HABIT

Watch the sunrise or sunset and remind yourself God is working.

**God's silence is not His absence; it is often His preparation.**

Let's get our worship on by singing "Light of the World" by Lauren Daigle.

God was not only preparing a miracle in Elizabeth. He was preparing a person for Mary. Before Mary ever walked through the door, God had already placed someone in her story who would believe her. Encourage her. Speak truth over her.

And when the moment comes, you won't just need faith to receive it; you will have the strength to carry it.

> CARRY THIS WITH YOU
>
> *Delay Is Not Denial.*

## LEARN IT. LIVE IT.

Let's practice your focus verse. Try to fill in the blanks.

*"____________ is she who has ____________ that the Lord would fulfill his ____________ to her!"*

*Luke 1:45*

# DAY 3: YOU'RE NOT CRAZY—GOD SAID THAT

**Focus Verse**

*"Blessed is she who has believed that the Lord would fulfill his promises to her!"*

*Luke 1:45*

There is something powerful about the right person showing up at the right time. My first year of college, I showed up with . . . let's just say some emotional baggage. Not the cute, organized carry-on kind. More like the overstuffed suitcase that won't zip, and you're sitting on it hoping for the best.

At the end of high school, I had gone through a breakup that felt like it belonged in a dramatic teen movie. My boyfriend started dating my best friend behind my back. So that was fun. Super fun. Highly recommend. (Kidding. Do not recommend.)

Needless to say, I came into college thinking, "Maybe I'll just not trust people for a while. You know, just keep things light. Friendly. No emotional investments. No expectations. No heartbreak." Solid plan.

And then God gently ignored my plan.

He placed a girl on my floor who happened to be in one of my classes. We started walking to class together, and within about five minutes, I realized—oh no. I like her. This is dangerous. She had this dry, sneaky sense of humor that would catch me off guard and make me laugh way harder than I intended. And slowly, without me even realizing it, walls started coming down. Before I knew it, we were doing everything together: walking to class, eating, studying, laughing at things that probably weren't even that funny. And just like that, God started healing something in me I didn't even know how to fix.

He gave me a friend who felt safe. A friend who saw me. A friend who didn't wound me but helped restore me. God provided the right person at exactly the right time.

Read Luke 1:39-40. What does Mary do after the angel leaves?

**God graciously led Mary to the very person who would strengthen her faith. God led Mary to the very place where her faith would be strengthened.**

Remember how Gabriel told Mary that her relative Elizabeth was already pregnant? So after the angel's appearance, Mary didn't stay where she was. She got up and she went. Scripture says she hurried to the hill country of Judea to visit Elizabeth. Not randomly. Not casually. Intentionally. Because when the angel told her about Elizabeth, it wasn't just information; it was direction. God graciously led Mary to the very person who would strengthen her faith. God led Mary to the very place where her faith would be strengthened.

She had almost one hundred miles to walk to Liz's house. The journey would have taken several days, maybe close to a week, traveling along dusty roads that wound through valleys and up into the rugged hill country. She likely joined a small group of travelers for safety, moving steadily by day and resting under the stars at night. With every step, she carried more than just the physical weight of the journey; she also carried questions, wonder, fear, and hope. What would Joseph say? What would people think? Could this really be happening? And somewhere along those miles, as her feet hit the ground step after step, her thoughts likely turned into prayers. Walking. Thinking. Praying. Repeating it all over again. And with each step forward, she wasn't just getting closer to Elizabeth. She was learning to trust the God who was leading her there.

Now read Luke 1:41-45. What happens when Elizabeth hears Mary's greeting?

What does Elizabeth say to Mary?

Don't you just love this? Liz's baby had a little dance party when Mary came near. Elizabeth hears Mary's voice, and the baby leaps with joy in her womb. This is a response to the presence of God as He comes near.

Elizabeth, filled with the Holy Spirit, begins to speak. Not opinions. Not guesses. *Holy Spirit truth.*

*"Blessed are you among women . . ."*

*"Blessed is the child you will bear . . ."*

*"Blessed is she who has believed . . ."*

## FAITH HABIT

Text one person something encouraging today.

Can you imagine this moment for Mary? She hasn't even said anything yet. She hasn't explained the angel. She hasn't told her story. And yet Elizabeth already *knows.* Another miracle. Another confirmation. Another layer of hope for Mary to carry.

Have you ever had a moment where someone spoke something over you and you just knew it was from God?

Mary walked in carrying something fragile. A promise she had just received. A calling she was still trying to understand. A future that probably felt both exciting and terrifying. And before she could even process it out loud, Elizabeth confirmed it. What a gift. She believed her. She blessed her. She spoke truth over her.

Mary didn't have to prove anything. She could take a deep breath and rest. This would be a safe place for her and the baby to rest. Mary's miracle stood in the presence of Elizabeth's miracle. What joy.

God rarely speaks to me directly, and I'm guessing it's the same for you. Instead, we hear His voice through the people surrounding us. Who are the voices in your life right now? Are they

- strengthening your faith?
- reminding you of what God has said?
- calling out what God is doing in you?

Or are they

- feeding your fear?
- increasing your doubt?
- pulling you away from what God has already spoken?

Enjoy this beautiful song: “The Light Has Come (Mary & Elizabeth’s Song)” featuring Ashley Corryn.

Mary needed Elizabeth, and God knew it. She needed someone who could recognize what God was doing and speak life into her. Liz helped to build Mary’s confidence and reassure her that she was not crazy for believing God. She could trust the miracle because she could see one. A visible, growing, undeniable miracle in Elizabeth.

Mary walked all those miles to see Liz as a walking miracle, testifying daily to God’s ability to do what no one thought was possible.

Remember, Elizabeth had been prepared for this moment. All those years of waiting, all those quiet prayers, all that unseen faithfulness—these things positioned her to recognize God’s work and speak truth at exactly the right time.

God had already placed in Mary’s path the exact voice she would need to hear. And He still does it today for us whom He calls his children.

Where might God be trying to confirm something in your life? Is there something He has already spoken that you need to hear again through someone else?

When truth is spoken over you, it strengthens you. When someone calls out what God is doing in your life, it anchors you. And when God confirms His promise, it gives you the strength to carry it.

CARRY THIS WITH YOU

*If God Said It, He’ll Confirm It.*

## LEARN IT. LIVE IT.

Let’s practice your focus verse. Try to fill in the blanks.

*“__________ is she who has __________ that the Lord would fulfill his __________ to her!”*

*Luke 1:45*

# DAY 4: WHEN GRATITUDE SNEAKS UP ON YOU

**Focus Verse**

*"Blessed is she who has believed that the Lord would fulfill his promises to her!"*
*Luke 1:45*

There can be a moment in parenting when you realize you are officially outnumbered. For me, it was after baby number three. We went from man-to-man defense to zone coverage. And I was not prepared.

We didn't have family nearby, which meant there was no "Hey Mom, can you just come over real quick?" option. It was just my husband and me and a whole lot of tiny humans with very big needs. I remember hitting a point where I thought, *We need some help.* So I started praying. Simple prayers. Honest prayers. Slightly desperate prayers. "God, I need help."

Not a five-year plan. Not a detailed strategy. Just help.

And then one day, I got a call from a woman at our church. A retired woman I barely knew. She said, "I've been praying and asking God to show me a family I could help, and I think He told me to call you." Excuse me . . . *what*??

She offered to come over once a week. Watch the baby. Let me take a nap. Help with laundry. I didn't even hesitate. I was like, "Yes. Yes, you can come over. In fact, do you want my address, my schedule, and possibly my firstborn?" (Kidding. Mostly.)

And just like that, every Monday, she showed up. She held babies. She folded laundry. She gave me space to breathe. And somewhere along the way, she became more than help. She became family. An adopted "Grammy" to our kids. A gift I didn't even know how to ask for.

Looking back, I am still so, so grateful. God didn't just meet a need; He overwhelmed me with kindness. She is one of the greatest blessings in my life—and my kids'. Not only does she pour into them with kindness and care, but also with Scripture and prayer.

And that's what God does. He doesn't just provide. He pours out. He fills our lives in ways we didn't even know to ask for. And we see that same kind of overflowing response in Mary.

**God doesn't just provide. He pours out. He fills our lives in ways we didn't even know to ask for.**

Read Luke 1:46-55. What is Mary's response after Elizabeth speaks over her?

Mary doesn't respond with fear. She doesn't spiral into questions. She doesn't start listing all the reasons this might not work. She sings.

> *"My soul glorifies the Lord and my spirit rejoices in God my Savior."*
> *(Luke 1:46-47)*

This is what happens when belief takes root. It turns into worship. Mary walked into Elizabeth's home unsure. But after hearing Elizabeth's words after experiencing that confirmation, she was at peace. And inspired. That faith, hope, and love began to overflow into a beautiful song of joy. Her gratitude for Elizabeth's kindness and God's faithfulness turned into worship.

Have you ever had a moment where God did something in your life and you didn't even have words for it at first? And then suddenly it turned into gratitude? Or into worship?

Mary declares what God is doing. Not just around her but in her.

> *"{F}or He has been mindful*
> *of the humble state of his servant…*
> *"The Mighty One has done great things for me."*
> *Luke 1:48-49*

**Worship is not based on having all the answers. It's based on trusting the One who does.**

She can't help magnifying God for His goodness. She is celebrating His power and the awe of being chosen by God to join Him in His good work. Mary doesn't have the full picture yet. She doesn't know how people will respond. She doesn't know how Joseph will react. And she has no clue how the story will unfold.

All she knows to do is praise. Because worship is not based on having all the answers. It's based on trusting the One who does.

Look up these verses on praise:

- Psalm 100:1-5
- Psalm 103:1-5
- Isaiah 12:4-5
- Philippians 4:4-7
- 1 Thessalonians 5:16-18
- Hebrews 13:15

Which verse stands out to you today? Why?

## FAITH HABIT

Tell someone what you're learning in this study.

Mary doesn't just say a prayer; she sings one. There is something powerful about songs in Scripture. When words aren't quite enough, songs carry what our hearts are trying to say. They help us remember what God has done, anchor us in what is true, and declare who He is—even when life still feels uncertain. Songs don't require everything to be resolved. They simply require a heart that is willing to respond.

And Mary isn't the first woman in Scripture to do this. Deborah did the same thing in Judges 5. After God gave victory to Israel, she didn't just acknowledge it; she sang about it. She declared it. She made sure it would be remembered. You can learn all about Deborah in *Not One Moment Late: Trusting God's Timing for Your Life.*

Songs become memorable for generations. A song could be sung and passed down to commemorate what God has done. Mary's song does this. She takes what God has done in her life and turns it into worship.

Just as God poured care and abundance into Mary through Elizabeth, God wants to do that for you. When the goodness of God becomes real to your heart, it does not stay contained. It rises as praise. He fills your life in such a way that it overflows.

Where have you seen God's kindness in your life recently? Big or small, where has He shown up?

**Get your worship on and sing "Gratitude" by Brandon Lake.**

What would it look like to respond the way Mary did? Not waiting until everything makes sense but choosing to worship right now?

When you begin to recognize what God is doing, gratitude grows, confidence builds, and worship flows.

Mary didn't just carry the promise. She carried the praise. Maybe that's part of what God is wanting to form in you right now. Not just the strength to carry what He's given you, but a heart that overflows with worship while you carry it.

> CARRY THIS WITH YOU
> *His Promise. My Peace.*

## LEARN IT. LIVE IT.

Fill in the blanks of this week's focus verse.

*"__________ is she who has __________ that the Lord would fulfill his __________ to her!"*

*Luke 1:45*

# DAY 5: BACK TO REAL LIFE (BUT DIFFERENT)

**Focus Verse**

*"Blessed is she who has believed that the Lord would fulfill his promises to her!"*

*Luke 1:45*

June. July. August. *Three glorious words.*

Summer. I love summer. I really do. As a kid, it meant school was out and we had three delicious months of freedom. No homework. No alarms. No packed lunches of bologna sandwiches.

My birthday is in June, and my mom has rhododendron bushes that always bloom right around that time. She called them the "*Lisa bushes*" while I was growing up, which, obviously, made me feel very important. Like the flowers and I had some kind of exclusive seasonal contract.

Nowadays, July is my favorite month. My two sisters and I pack up our families and head to the lake for a couple of weeks. It's chaos—in the best way. There are kids everywhere, towels everywhere, and somehow no one can ever find a matching pair of flip-flops. We're boating, swimming, sailing, and eating *an unknown amount of good food.* Ice cream runs. Fireworks. Bonfires. Late-night talks. It's loud. It's messy. It's slightly sticky at all times.

And I love every second of it.

And then August rolls in with slower days. Beach walks. Lingering sunsets. That feeling of wanting to soak up every last drop before life picks up speed again.

Three months. Full. Joyful. Memorable.

But here's the thing about those three months: They don't last forever. Eventually, summer ends. We pack up. We head home. And we step back into real life.

And that's exactly where we find Mary.

Read Luke 1:56:

*"Mary stayed with Elizabeth for about three months and then returned home."*

Often the early months of pregnancy are kept quiet until the twelve-week mark has passed. It is a tender, uncertain season. A time of waiting, watching, and protecting what's growing before it becomes fully visible.

Mary had just experienced one of the most powerful seasons of her life. Three months with Elizabeth. Three months of confirmation. Three months of encouragement. Three months of watching God's promises grow, literally, in both of their lives. It was a sacred season. The first trimester was over. Mary's baby bump was starting to show. She was getting her energy back. She could keep down more than saltines. Her faith was rock solid. Her calling was affirmed. It was time to return home.

Back to reality. . . . But a whole new, life-forever-changed reality. What would a new normal look like for the mother of the Son of God? Mary couldn't stay with Elizabeth forever. She had to move beyond that safe comfort zone and take a stand. For herself. For her baby. For her future.

She went back.

**Faith isn't just something you have in the safe places. It's the kind of trust you live out in the real ones.**

Back to Nazareth. Back to real life. Back to questions. Back to people who wouldn't understand. Back to a future she couldn't fully explain. Why? Because faith isn't just something you have in the safe places. It's the kind of trust you live out in the real ones. Mary was carrying a promise that was not for her alone. It was for all her people. It was the fulfilled promise of the Jewish people. Did Mary know that it was not just for them, but for all of humanity?

If you've ever gone to a Christian retreat or camp, you might have had what we sometimes call a "mountaintop experience." But then it ends, and we have to come back down. Back to the same life. Back to the same family and friends. Back to the same jobs. Back to a situation that doesn't make sense. Maybe even back to hard and difficult settings.

Can you think of a time in your life when this was true for you?

Perseverance begins in the moment of the return. That takes your foundation of faith and deepens your dependence on God. The emotions that may carry us when things are going well can quickly be challenged. It is in the hard moments that we look back to the foundation of God's faithfulness to give us solid footing.

Mary did not know what came next. But she took the next step. Actually, she took a whole lot of steps back to Nazareth—about 250,000 steps!

## FAITH HABIT

Play worship music and, if able, stand for one full song.

What would it look like to move forward in obedience, even if you don't feel fully ready?

Look up these verses on continuing what God begins:

- Philippians 1:6
- Psalm 37:23-24
- Matthew 25:23
- John 15:4-5
- Hebrews 12:1-2

What does it look like to keep going when a season changes? Which verse stands out to you today? Why?

Mary's story reminds us that faith doesn't *end* with a "yes." It *begins* with a "yes" and continues with a walk. A daily, steady, sometimes uncertain but always surrendered walk with God.

Mary returned home carrying more than a promise. She carried strengthened faith, confirmed truth, and a deep trust in the God who had

Get your worship on and sing "Take You at Your Word" by Cody Carnes.

called her. The quiet months with Elizabeth had prepared her heart for what was ahead—but they had not removed the reality of what was coming next.

Because while Mary knew what God had spoken, not everyone else did. There were still conversations to be had. Still questions to be answered. Still a future that would unfold in ways she could not yet see. And one of the most important parts of her story was just beginning.

Her life with Joseph.

A man who had his own plans. His own expectations. And his own decision to make. Because sometimes, when God is writing a story, He isn't just working in you. He's working in the people around you too.

> CARRY THIS WITH YOU
> *What God Begins, He Completes.*

## LEARN IT. LIVE IT.

Fill in the blanks of this week's focus verse.

*"____________ is she who has ____________ that the Lord would fulfill his ____________ to her!"*

*Luke 1:45*

# VIDEO VIEWER GUIDE: WEEK 2

God rarely gives a calling without also sending ________________.

God strengthens us through the ________ He places around us.

Be an ____________ for someone else.

Mary turns her focus from her circumstances to God's ___________.

What we magnify determines what feels ___________ in our lives.

Our strength comes from confidence in the ____________ of God.

# DISCUSSION QUESTIONS: WEEK 2

- Lisa shared about switching from a real Christmas tree to an artificial one. What is a small tradition or expectation you had growing up that didn't turn out quite the way you imagined in adulthood?
- Have you ever had a season where you felt like you were carrying something heavy or unexpected–like the backpack Lisa described? What made that season challenging?
- Mary was strengthened when Elizabeth recognized what God was doing in her life. Has there ever been someone who encouraged or confirmed God's work in your life during a difficult season?
- Mary responded by worshipping and magnifying God in the Magnificat. Why do you think focusing on God's character can strengthen us when our circumstances feel overwhelming?
- Where might God be inviting you this week to either receive encouragement–or be an "Elizabeth" for someone else who needs strength?
- What is one thing you are carrying right now that you could intentionally bring to God in prayer this week?

# WEEK 3

# STEADY

## Glory and Peace

### FOCUS VERSE

*For my eyes have seen your salvation, which you have prepared in the sight of all nations.*

*Luke 2:30-31*

# Take Action

## A Little Mary-ment

What do you call a sheep who was at the first Christmas?

A witness to the greatest baa-by ever born.

HA HA HA

LOL

## SERVE

Serve some Christmas tea to your small group or a group of friends. Say one thing you appreciate about each one of them.

# Steady

## Creation Corner

Stand quietly outside and close your eyes. Feel the wind on your face and listen to the sound it makes in the trees or grass. You cannot see the wind, but you can feel its movement. God's Spirit often moves in ways we cannot see but can deeply feel. Where have you sensed God gently leading you lately?

Read John 3:8

## CREATE

String together a popcorn and cranberry garland for your tree, mantel, or hang it outside as a nutritious outdoor feeder for winter wildlife, or a completely compostable holiday craft!

# Moments with Mary

*But Mary treasured up all these things and pondered them in her heart.*
*Luke 2:19*

Bethlehem is crowded tonight. Travelers from every direction have filled the narrow streets because of the census ordered by Caesar Augustus. Donkeys bray, merchants call out to one another, and families hurry through the town searching for a place to stay.

Joseph and I arrived exhausted after the long journey from Nazareth. Each mile along the dusty road had become more difficult as the child I carried within me grew heavier. By the time the houses of Bethlehem came into view, my body was aching and weary.

Joseph found a place for us to stay that was quiet. There was no guest room for us, but a simple space that had a manger was available.

And tonight, it became the place where my son entered the world. The labor pains came quickly once we were inside. Women usually give birth surrounded by mothers and midwives, but here it was only Joseph and me in the dim light of a small oil lamp. The smell of hay and animals filled the air as the hours passed.

And then, at last, my baby was born. I was in awe. A perfect little human. I'm not sure what I expected, but he had ten perfect little fingers and ten little toes. He cried, yawned, looking at me before closing his eyes in sleep. I was a mother. As I held his tiny hand, I knew I would do anything for him.

Joseph wrapped him carefully in the clothes we had brought from Nazareth, and I laid Jesus in a manger filled with fresh straw.

The Son of God. Could it really be?

Jesus. The One who saves. As I held my son close tonight, the words of the prophet returned to me:

> *"But you, Bethlehem Ephrathah, . . .*
> *out of you will come for me*
> *one who will be ruler over Israel."*
>
> Micah 5:2

I am living out the prophecies of old. I am part of this story. This is nothing like the life I imagined for myself, but whatever comes next, I know I will never forget these moments.

And I know that the God who brought Jesus to me will also give me the strength to carry whatever is ahead.

Mary

# DAY 1: WHEN NOTHING MAKES SENSE BUT GOD IS WORKING

**Focus Verse**

> *"Glory to God in the highest heaven,*
> *and on earth peace to those on whom his favor rests."*
> *Luke 2:14*

I didn't get into my first-choice college. I was bummed. And I took it just a *tiny bit* personally. Don't you want me at your school?

I'm not talking mildly disappointed. Not like, "Oh well, that's okay." No. I was like, *How could you not see my potential?* I had already pictured it. The campus. The friends. The future. My whole life was basically planned out in my seventeen-year-old brain—which, as we all know, is the most reliable life-planning system available.

So when the rejection came, I was crushed. Confused. Slightly dramatic. Definitely questioning the admissions team's life choices. Whatever. Their loss.

So I did what any mature, emotionally stable teenager would do: I pivoted hard. I said yes to my second-choice school. I committed. I started preparing. I told people, "This is where I'm going," like I had always meant to do that. And then . . .

My first-choice college called me. "Hey! Good news! A spot opened up—we'd love to offer it to you." *Oh, now we're interested?* And I had a moment. A real moment. Because this was the dream, right? This was what I had wanted all along. But instead of an enthusiastic *yes*, I was like, "Um, no thank you." I had already moved on. I had already made plans down a different path. And I think I even sensed that maybe, just maybe, God had something for me there.

And He did. I *loved* where I went to school. God met me there. He grew me. He stretched me. I built incredible friendships. And I even got a few semesters with my younger sister, which was an absolute blast.

Looking back, what felt like rejection was actually redirection. What felt like a closed door was God strengthening me to walk through a different one. I had no idea what God was up to. God was strengthening me before I understood what He was doing. Oh, it definitely did not feel like strength in the moment. It was big-time disappointment. Confusion.

And that's exactly where we meet Joseph. Not at the miracle. Not at the wonder. Not in clarity. Not at the moment where everything makes sense. We meet him in the middle of the unknown. A moment where everything he thought his life would look like suddenly disappears. A moment where his plans are interrupted, his future feels uncertain, and the story in front of him doesn't add up. And before God explains anything, before God gives clarity, before Joseph understands the bigger picture . . . God begins to strengthen him.

Read Matthew 1:18-19. What do we learn about Joseph?

What situation is Joseph facing?

Joseph had a plan. He was a faithful Jewish man. Honorable. Steady. The kind of guy people respected. He was engaged to Mary, preparing for marriage, building a home, and stepping into his future. And then everything suddenly changed. Mary was pregnant. And Joseph knew one thing for sure: the child was not his.

I'm not sure how Mary told him. Maybe softly. Maybe tearfully. Maybe with trembling faith. But however it happened, the moment had to land hard. Shock. Heartbreak. Confusion. How could she do this? How could this happen? What was he supposed to do?

Matthew tells us that Joseph was faithful to the Law, and yet he did not want to expose Mary to public disgrace. So he planned to divorce her quietly.

In the first-century Jewish world, betrothal was a legal covenant. To break it required divorce. In a situation like this, Joseph had options. He could have handled this publicly. He could have made it known that he was not responsible.

That would have protected his reputation and placed the full weight of shame on Mary.[1]

But Matthew tells us something different about Joseph. He was faithful to the Law, *and* he did not want to expose her to public disgrace. So he made a decision. Not to ignore what had happened. Not to pretend it didn't matter. But to step away quietly. This was Joseph revealing that he was a man of character. Honestly, it shows what kind of man Mary would have with her to carry the weight of raising the Son of God.

Joseph was revealing himself as a man of righteousness without retaliation.[2] He was modeling justice without cruelty. This would be the character of the earthly father who would raise Jesus with Mary. Joseph did not throw around blame or shame or demand that everyone see that he was right. He chose restraint.

And that kind of strength? That kind of strength doesn't come naturally. That is the kind of strength God is forming in him for the road ahead—even before Joseph understands what God is doing. Joseph's response shows us a kind of strength that isn't loud or obvious. It's quiet. Steady. Controlled. Rooted in trust.

Let's see this kind of strength echoed throughout Scripture. Look up these verses and jot down any thoughts on what they reveal about strength, restraint, and trusting God when you don't understand.

- Proverbs 16:32
- James 1:19-20
- Romans 12:17-19
- Psalm 37:7-9
- 2 Corinthians 12:7-10
- Isaiah 40:29-31

In the midst of pain and confusion, he was trying to be honorable by keeping things quiet. His world didn't make sense, and he tried to step away. It was too much, more than he could handle. This was not what he signed up for.

Have you ever had a moment where your plans suddenly didn't make sense anymore? Where something shifted—and you were left trying to figure out what to do next?

Joseph didn't have the full story. Maybe Mary told him about the angel, the miracle, the promise. Even the amazing God-story of Liz and Zech. But it was just all too much for him. All he knew was that his life no longer looked the way he thought it would.

Sometimes, God is strengthening you before He ever explains anything to you.

I don't like being kept in the dark on things. I want to be in the know. But God often grows us in the moments of uncertainty. Trust is something that grows only in the belief that God will come through for us when we don't know what to do.

**God often grows us in the moments of uncertainty.**

We often think strength looks like confidence. If we feel good about something and have a plan, we feel more capable. We have our next steps mapped out, and that makes us feel a little more in control.

But biblical strength often looks very different. It looks like leaning into God when you feel weak. Trusting Him when you don't have clarity. Holding steady when everything inside of you wants answers. This is the kind of strength that leans into God and trusts Him when we feel weak. Peace doesn't always come when life is clear.

Another follower of Jesus, Paul, gave this advice to the Philippians about God's peace:

> *And the peace of God, which transcends all understanding, will guard your hearts and your minds in Christ Jesus.*
>
> *Philippians 4:7*

### FAITH HABIT

Open your hands and say out loud, "God, I trust You with this."

**Get your worship on with Katy Nichole singing "O What a King."**

Peace that doesn't make sense. Peace that shows up before clarity. Peace that guards your heart—even in the unknown. And that's the kind of strength God was forming in Joseph.

And it's the kind of strength He is forming in you.

> CARRY THIS WITH YOU
> *Unexpected Doesn't Mean Unplanned.*

## LEARN IT. LIVE IT.

Fill in the blanks:

*"Glory to ______ in the ____________ heaven,*
*and on earth ________ to those on whom his __________ rests."*

*Luke 2:14*

# DAY 2: WHEN GOD FINALLY SPEAKS

**Focus Verse**

*"Glory to God in the highest heaven,*
*and on earth peace to those on whom his favor rests."*
*Luke 2:14*

Have you ever had one of those nights where you just can't sleep? You're tired. Your body is ready. But your mind? Wide awake. Running laps. Replaying conversations. Asking questions that don't have answers, yet. You roll over. Check the clock. Why is it always 2:17 a.m.? You try to pray but it turns into thinking. You try to rest, but it turns into worrying.

Why does time crawl so darn slowly at night when we can't sleep? We toss and turn and know that tomorrow is going to be painful with no sleep. Sometimes the quiet is very, very loud.

And sometimes it takes that loud quiet to create enough room for God to speak. That is what happened to Joseph. I can only imagine that he had some sleepless nights trying to figure out what to do when Mary returned to Nazareth pregnant. God revealed Himself to Joseph through an angel in a dream.

Read Matthew 1:20-23. What happens while Joseph is sleeping?

What does the angel say to him?

What name is given to the child, and what does it mean?

"Joseph son of David, do not be afraid " (Matthew 1:20). Do you remember what the angel also told Mary? "Do not be afraid, Mary" (Luke 1:30).

What a powerful affirmation that God knew there was a lot of fear. Fear of being in the presence of an angel. Fear about what was being asked of them. Fear for the future. Fear of the responsibility. What message did God want them to play over and over in their minds? Do not be afraid. God addresses the fear first.

**When we let fear take the lead, God often reminds us that we need to recenter our faith on Him.**

Fear comes from living in the unknown and not being in control. That is right smack-dab in the middle of where we all live. So how do we live without fear? That is the offer that God has for us. Exchange fear for faith. Faith that God is in control. Faith that God has a good plan. Faith that God can be trusted with your life. When we let fear take the lead, God often reminds us that we need to recenter our faith on Him.

How do you think faith helps us fight fear?

Let's look at another place in Scripture that talks about fear:

*So do not fear, for I am with you;*
*do not be dismayed, for I am your God.*
*I will strengthen you and help you;*
*I will uphold you with my righteous right hand.*
*Isaiah 41:10*

God truly was with Mary and Joseph. He sent His angels to be His messengers. Joseph saw the angel in a dream. Sometimes in Scripture, dreams were one way God communicated with His people (Joseph [son of Jacob], Jacob, Solomon, Joseph [husband of Mary], and Daniel), especially when He was guiding them into something significant. Joseph, like others before him, receives direction from God not in a public moment, but in a personal one. This was not an ambiguous fuzzy dream that left Joseph uncertain of its meaning; rather, it was a clear word from God. He gave Joseph what he needed most:

Truth.

*"Do not be afraid to take Mary home as your wife . . ."*
*"What is conceived in her is from the Holy Spirit . . ."*
*"You are to give him the name Jesus . . ."*
*"He will save his people from their sins . . ."*

God spoke directly into Joseph's confusion with clarity about who He is and what He was doing. And that's what God's Word does. God's Word doesn't answer every question, but it anchors us in what is true.

Look up these verses and notice what God's Word does in moments of uncertainty:

- Psalm 119:105
- Hebrews 4:12
- Romans 10:17
- 2 Timothy 3:16-17
- 1 Corinthians 2:13

Which one speaks to you most right now?

Joseph didn't move forward because he suddenly felt confident. He moved forward because God had spoken. He trusted God.

Have you ever had a moment where God brought a verse to mind at just the right time? Or someone spoke truth over you that you knew was exactly what you needed to hear?

God still speaks.

Through His Word. Through His Spirit. Through truth that anchors you when everything else feels uncertain.

## FAITH HABIT

Write your fear on paper and replace it with a truth from God.

Let's get our worship on with "Trust in You" by Lauren Daigle.

Joseph went to sleep in confusion, but he woke up with direction. Everything was not resolved simply because God had spoken. However, sometimes one word from God is enough to take our next step.

> CARRY THIS WITH YOU
> *God Will Make a Way Through This.*

## LEARN IT. LIVE IT.

Fill in the blanks:

*"Glory to ______ in the ___________ heaven,*
*and on earth ________ to those on whom his __________ rests."*

*Luke 2:14*

# DAY 3: YOU DON'T HAVE TO DO THIS ALONE

**Focus Verse**

> *"Glory to God in the highest heaven,*
> *and on earth peace to those on whom his favor rests."*
> *Luke 2:14*

I moved to California for graduate school and was stepping a bit into the unknown. But I did at least line up a place to stay. I had arranged to live in an apartment with someone who went to the same college as me—which sounds promising, right? Except for the small detail that we didn't actually know each other. So I drove all the way from Michigan, thinking, I'll just get furniture when I get there. Very optimistic. Very confident. Very incorrect.

I opened the door to my new room, and . . . nothing. No bed. No chair. No desk. Just me. Standing there like, *Well this is minimalism at its finest.* Meanwhile, my roommate was living her best life—busy with her boyfriend, school, and a full California calendar. And I was like, "Cool, cool, cool. I'll just be over here sitting on the floor," which, by the way, gets old surprisingly fast.

Thankfully, God knew I needed help before I was permanently committed to floor living. A couple I had met during my visit to the school reached out and said they wanted to help me get settled. And when I say help, I mean they came through.

They donated an oversized armchair that leaned just slightly to one side—which meant every time I sat in it, I felt like I was slowly sliding into a nap. Honestly? Still a win. Then they took me to get a bed, helped me load it, drove it back, and carried it into my apartment like absolute heroes.

Add in a donated dresser, and suddenly I had a home. Looking back, I am so grateful. Because yes—you can do some things alone. But the hard things? Those are a whole lot better when others show up to help you carry them.

After Joseph's encounter with God, he was in. Mary had his support. They were now in this together. She had the protection and companionship of Joseph.

**FAITH HABIT**

Thank God out loud for five things you already have.

Read Matthew 1:24-25.

Joseph went through with the wedding and took Mary as his wife. Good job, Joe! We are cheering you both on. This was a pretty big deal because Joseph didn't just make a private decision; he also made a public one. Weddings would be family and village-wide celebrations. Joseph didn't just believe God in his heart—through his commitment to Mary, he aligned his life with what God said. That kind of obedience is costly. Joseph knew it and did it anyway.

Mary comes back into focus in such a powerful way. Mary had already said yes to God. She had already believed the impossible. She had already carried the calling. But now? She had her husband standing beside her. He believed her. He believed God. He was ready to do this hard thing with her. Together they were going to parent Jesus, the Son of God! Joseph's decision shaped how Mary would live in her world.

God gave Joseph the strength to step into a life he did not choose. The strength that He gave Joseph was not for him alone. It was also for Mary and their future son, Jesus. Sometimes the strength that you find that God has given you isn't just for yourself. It's for others as well.

**Sometimes the strength that you find that God has given you isn't just for yourself. It's for others as well.**

Let's look at some other places in Scripture that encourage us about what love in action looks like:

- Ecclesiastes 4:9-12
- Galatians 6:2
- Romans 12:10-13
- Mark 10:43-44
- James 2:8

Which one of these speaks most to your life today? What do you think God wants to say to you through His Word?

Have you ever had someone show up for you at just the right time? Not to fix everything, but to stand with you?

**Ready to get your worship on? Let's sing "Manger Throne" with Phil Wickham.**

God often strengthens us through people. Through someone who stays. Through someone who believes. Through someone who chooses to walk with us.

And just like Mary, sometimes the strength you need comes in the form of someone God sends. Joseph didn't just hear from God. He responded. And his obedience became part of Mary's strength. Mary and Joseph together decided not to step into comfort, but into calling.

Following God should not be private. It shows up in your choices. Your relationships. Your decisions. Sometimes, not everyone will understand. But obedience isn't about pleasing others. It's about understanding God's will and being faithful to Him.

> CARRY THIS WITH YOU
>
> *Follow God Now. He'll Explain Later.*

## LEARN IT. LIVE IT.

Fill in the blanks:

*"Glory to ________ in the ______________ heaven,*
*and on earth __________ to those on whom his ____________ rests."*

*Luke 2:14*

# DAY 4: THIS IS NOT HOW I PLANNED IT

**Focus Verse**

*"Glory to God in the highest heaven,*
*and on earth peace to those on whom his favor rests."*
*Luke 2:14*

I've had the privilege of visiting Bethlehem, the location of Jesus's birth, several times, and I never get over it. There is something surreal about standing in the place where Mary and Joseph traveled. Like this is it. This is the town. The real one. Not the nativity set version with perfectly placed figurines and sheep.

Right in the center of Bethlehem is the Church of the Nativity. The church is located on the traditional site where Jesus is believed to have been born. If you ever travel there, you may have to adjust expectations, because it is not a cute little stable or a cozy cave with straw all around. It is a massive, dark, ancient church crowded with thousands of pilgrims every single day.

But here's my favorite part: the door.

The entrance to the church is about half the size of a normal door. I'm not exaggerating. You cannot walk in like a normal, confident human being. You have to stop, bend over, and bow low to get through the door. Then pray that you don't bonk your head when you stand back up straight.

Very humbling.

Which, it turns out, was the point. The doorway was intentionally designed that way so that every single person who enters must bow. Not accidentally. Not symbolically. But physically.

The baby is no longer there. The manger is gone. But the reverence? It remains. People still come. People still bow. People still remember. I hope we always will.

Mary and Joseph were about to begin their journey from Nazareth to Bethlehem. Mary and Joseph didn't walk into comfort. They walked into a place that would require humility, surrender, and trust with every step.

Read Luke 2:1-5. What caused Mary and Joseph to travel?

Where did they have to go?

Caesar Augustus called for a count of the people in his kingdom so that Rome could figure out how many people to tax.[3] The Romans built empires, kept records, and loved to issue taxes to fund their huge army. Caesar Augustus, the first emperor, almost doubled the empire's size.[4] Rome dominated the region from Great Britain to India. Spain, Italy, Greece, Egypt, North Africa, Asia Minor, and the Near East were all part of the Roman Empire. It was massive. Rome controlled all of the land that bordered the Mediterranean Sea.[5]

Israel was no longer ruled by judges or kings. The last king of Judah was conquered by Babylon in 586 BCE.[6] Many Jews were taken into captivity in Babylon. Some returned when King Cyrus of Persia allowed them to rebuild Jerusalem in 538 BCE. But Israel remained under the control of Persia and then Greece. They did gain a few years of freedom under the Hasmoneans, a Jewish dynasty, but then were conquered again by Rome in 63 BCE.[7]

During the time of Mary and Joseph, Israel was thought of as a drop in the bucket in the huge Roman mega-kingdom. The Jews had enough autonomy[8] within Rome's rule that they could hold on to their religious customs as their way of life. Some Jews were Roman citizens (like Paul)[9] and held more rights and privileges, but most were not. The Jews paid taxes to Rome[10] and followed Roman law, so they had to follow the decrees of Caesar Augustus about the census.

Have you ever had something interrupt your life that you didn't ask for?

**FAITH HABIT**

Start your day with "I am loved. I am chosen. I am His."

The journey from Nazareth to Bethlehem was roughly one hundred miles. For Mary to travel at the end stages of pregnancy would have been slow going. It likely took them a week to travel the distance while making comfort stops for the restroom and food. This was not the babymoon she was likely daydreaming about.

All these events took place as part of God's plan. Did you know there was prophecy written in the Old Testament about Bethlehem? It's true! Check it out.

Read Micah 5:2. Where did the Messiah need to be born?

Yes. You got it. Bethlehem. This was King David's hometown, and it made sense that the expected Jewish king, the Messiah, would come from David's family tree and be born in his hometown. It was a prophecy waiting to be fulfilled, and Caesar unknowingly was fulfilling it.[11] So what looked like a random government decision was actually God moving the story exactly where it needed to be. God used a decree from a Roman emperor to move two ordinary people to the exact place where the prophecy would be fulfilled. Mary and Joseph probably didn't see that in their travel. They just felt the weight of the journey.

Look up these verses:

- Proverbs 16:9
- Isaiah 55:8-9
- Matthew 7:7-8
- Romans 8:28
- James 4:15

What do these verses reveal about God's plans versus ours?

God is not limited by our timelines. He is not thrown off by detours. He is not scrambling to fix what feels off track to us. He is already working. Even in the disruption.

**God is not limited by our timelines.**

Mary and Joseph thought they were walking to Bethlehem because of a census. But they were really walking to Bethlehem because God was at work. God can send angels, create miraculous pregnancies, and even work with the government!

Sometimes the very thing we wish we could change is the thing that God is going to use to get us where we need to be. God's timing is not our own. God's plans are better than anything we could ever try to put into motion.

**Get your worship on with Matthew West singing "Because of Bethlehem."**

> CARRY THIS WITH YOU
> *Hope Has a Name.*

## LEARN IT. LIVE IT.

Fill in the blanks:

*"Glory to ______ in the ___________ heaven,*
*and on earth ________ to those on whom his __________ rests."*

*Luke 2:14*

# DAY 5: WELL, THAT WASN'T WHAT I EXPECTED

**Focus Verse**

*"Glory to God in the highest heaven,*
*and on earth peace to those on whom his favor rests."*
*Luke 2:14*

We were very excited to visit San Francisco. Like tourist mode fully activated. Sourdough bread at the pier? Yes, please. Trolleys climbing those wild hills? Amazing. Golden Gate Bridge? Iconic. Ten out of ten.

And then there was Alcatraz. I had been waiting for this one. The famous prison on an island. The history. The stories. The drama. You have to take a boat to get there, which only increases the drama. Oh, this is going to be an experience.

So we step off the boat, taking it all in. Feeling very reflective. Feeling the history. Very National Geographic. And then, out of nowhere . . .

A seagull.

Decided.

To ruin my life.

I kid you not. Target. Aim. Fire. Direct hit. On my head. I just stood there for a second like, Did that really just happen? Is this part of the tour?

And suddenly, the whole experience shifted. I was no longer thinking about history or architecture or prison escapes. I was thinking, "I need a bathroom. Immediately. And possibly a new identity."

**The birth of Jesus, the most significant moment in history, did not unfold the way anyone would have imagined.**

It was not how I imagined the moment going. At all.

Have you ever had something you were looking forward to play out completely different from what you expected? Not necessarily bad. Just not what you pictured. That's the tension of this moment in the story. Because the birth of Jesus, the most significant moment in history, did not unfold the way anyone would have imagined.

No spotlight. No celebration. No perfect setting. Just something unexpected. And yet, it was exactly where God chose to show up.

Read Luke 2:6-7. What happens while Mary and Joseph are in Bethlehem?

Where is Jesus laid after He is born?

This is the moment everything has been building toward. The angel's announcement. Mary's "yes." Joseph's obedience. The long journey. And when it finally happens, it's not how anyone would expect heaven's King to arrive here on earth.

Where was the fanfare, the parades, the fireworks? It was just a brand-new mom, an earthly dad, and a heavenly Father with their newborn. In a space that was hastily found but gratefully received. It's not how I would have written the arrival of the Savior of the world. It was a little too ordinary. But it was exactly how God had planned.

Have you ever expected God to show up one way, and He showed up completely differently?

Where in your life might you be missing what God is doing because life doesn't look the way you want it to right now?

FAITH HABIT

Do one hard thing for five minutes you've been avoiding.

Jesus wasn't just born in a humble place. Mary didn't have a perfect setting. She didn't have a crowd. She didn't have comfort. But she had Jesus.

But before the shepherds arrived . . .

Before the angels filled the sky . . .

Before anyone else understood what was happening . . .

God had already told them something incredibly important.

A name.

Read Matthew 1:20-23 again. What name was Joseph told to give the child?

Why was this name to be given?

The name *Jesus* comes from the Hebrew name *Yeshua* (Joshua), which means "The Lord saves." This was a name filled with history and purpose. In the Jewish world, names mattered. A name wasn't just what you called someone. A name revealed identity, heritage, and calling.

So before Jesus ever took His first breath, God declared what He came to do. Not just to teach. Not just to heal. Not just to lead.

But to save.

From sin. From separation. From everything that stood between humanity and God.

Matthew 1:23 says that His name is also to be Immanuel, which means "God with us." Matthew connects this moment all the way back to prophecy:

> *"Therefore the Lord himself will give you a sign: The virgin will conceive and give birth to a son, and will call him Immanuel."*
>
> *Isaiah 7:14*

This is huge. For generations, God's presence had been experienced in specific places. In the Tabernacle. In the Temple. Through priests. Through prophets. And now? God wasn't just nearby. He was here, in flesh and blood.

Jesus tells us what He came to do. Immanuel tells us who He is. He is the God who saves and the God who stays.

Get your worship on with Stanaj and Tommee Profitt with "Noel (He Is Born)."

**CARRY THIS WITH YOU**
*Awe Leads to Action.*

## LEARN IT. LIVE IT.

Fill in the blanks:

*"Glory to ______ in the ____________ heaven,*
*and on earth _________ to those on whom his ___________ rests."*

*Luke 2:14*

# VIDEO VIEWER GUIDE: WEEK 3

She walked that _____ out on dusty roads–step by step.

Faith sometimes looks less like a moment . . . and more like a long walk of ___________.

But now she has to live inside the ____________ God gave her.

Mary remained __________.

Sometimes, inconvenience is ____________ where God is working.

Faithfulness is often formed in ________ moments.

God does some of His greatest work in places that look completely _____________.

Faith is trusting God when life still requires ____________.

Hidden _____________________ is never hidden from God.

He usually reveals the next _______.

It is lived in __________ obedience.

# DISCUSSION QUESTIONS: WEEK 3

- Lisa described the crowded, chaotic experience of Bethlehem during the Journey to Bethlehem event. Have you ever been part of a big event, trip, or holiday that didn't feel calm or peaceful at all, but was still memorable? What made it memorable?

- Mary and Joseph traveled about ninety miles to Bethlehem, likely walking many days in simple sandals. What part of Mary and Joseph's journey to Bethlehem stands out to you the most when you imagine what that trip might have been like?

- Lisa said, "Faith sometimes looks less like a moment . . . and more like a long walk of obedience." Can you think of a season in your life where faith felt more like a long journey than a single decision?

- Mary had already said yes to God, but life didn't suddenly become easier. Why do you think it can be difficult to keep trusting God when obedience leads to inconvenience or uncertainty?

- Luke says Mary "treasured up all these things and pondered them in her heart." What do you think it looks like in real life to remain steady in faith when circumstances feel chaotic or unclear?

- Lisa ended by asking the question: "Lord, what is the next faithful step you want me to take today?" What might be one "next faithful step" God could be inviting you to take in this season of your life?

# Week 4

# SUSTAINED

## Keep Your Eyes Open

## FOCUS VERSE

*For my eyes have seen your salvation,*
*which you have prepared in the*
*sight of all nations*

Luke 2:30-31

# Take Action

## A Little Mary-ment

Why did the shepherds run to Bethlehem instead of walking?

Because the angel said, "Hurry! This news is shear joy!

HA HA HA

LOL

## SERVE

Go shopping for an agricultural gift for a person in a developing country and make it a stocking stuffer.

HEIFER INTERNATIONAL

# Sustained

## Creation Corner

Find a tree and sit beneath it for five minutes. Look up through the branches and watch how the light moves through the leaves. Trees grow slowly, year by year, ring by ring. Most of the growth happens where we cannot see it. God often works in our lives the same way—slow, steady, and unseen. Where might God be growing something in you that others cannot see yet?

Read Psalm 1:3

## CREATE

Make some paper bag stars! Gather a variety of paper bags, brown and white. Add glue to the back of each bag, along the bottom, and up the center. Stack another bag on top (facing the same direction), press it in place, and continue adding glue and bags. Once you have all the bags glued together, cut the tops of the bags off, forming a point. Open the bags to make sure the ends meet.

# Moments with Mary

*But Mary treasured up all these things and pondered them in her heart.*
*Luke 2:19*

We drifted off to sleep until we were awakened by a group of shepherds who mysteriously found us. They arrived breathless and wide-eyed. They told us angels had appeared in their fields, singing and proclaiming the arrival of the Savior of this world. I knew then and there that I was not dreaming. There were miracles happening all around us. This baby was special. My heart swelled with wonder and love.

Morning light slipped quietly through the doorway. Dust floated in the air like tiny stars as the town of Bethlehem slowly stirred to life outside. Somewhere down the road, I could hear merchants opening their stalls and travelers beginning their journeys again.

But inside this small space, everything felt still. My baby slept peacefully in my arms, his tiny fingers curled around the edge of my robe. His breathing was soft and steady, and every so often his small face would move as if he were dreaming.

I am a mother now. Months ago, I was a girl from Nazareth preparing for marriage and an ordinary life. Now I hold my child whom the angel promised—the Son of the Most High. God.

There is joy in my soul, but there are also questions. What kind of life will this child live? What road will God ask him to walk? And what will it mean for me to be his mother? I do not know the answers.

Yet as I watch him sleep, peace settles gently over my heart. The God who placed this child in my arms will not leave me alone to raise him. The Psalms that I learned as a little girl return to my mind:

> The LORD is my strength and my shield;
> my heart trusts in him.
>
> Psalm 28:7a

I did not choose this path. But I trust the One who chose it for me. And somehow, in ways I cannot yet see, God will give me the strength to carry the deep love and hope that has been placed in my heart. And I sense this is only the beginning.

Already, shepherds have come with stories of angels and glory. Heaven is speaking. The message is spreading. I do not know who else God will send, or what words will be spoken over this child, but I know now that He is making Him known. This story is not staying small. It is reaching beyond us.

I will be there for Jesus—through the good and the hard. I will raise Him. I will care for him. I will carry Him.

Knowing that one day He will carry us all.

*Mary*

# DAY 1: DON'T MISS IT: GOD IS RIGHT HERE

**Focus Verse**

*"For my eyes have seen your salvation,*
*which you have prepared in the sight of all nations."*
*Luke 2:30-31*

I planned my first big event at my first big church ministry job, and I was feeling very confident about it. Like this is it. This is my moment. People are going to come. Lives are going to be changed. Also, there will be shopping.

I had this whole idea. A Christmas shopping outing for women. Festive. Fun. Helpful. I even arranged childcare at the church so moms could drop off their kids and shop in peace, which, honestly, should have guaranteed a million or two people—give or take.

No sign-ups. No pressure. Just show up at the church on Saturday morning, and we'll carpool together. Easy peasy. I drove there that morning with Christmas music at full volume. Like Amy Grant was basically cohosting this event with me.

I got there early with my morning coffee, watching the parking lot, ready to greet the crowds. And then a car pulled in. Yes! It's happening. I smiled. I waved. She got out, walked over, and joined me on the church steps. And then we waited. And waited. And waited.

I kept doing that thing where you pretend you're not checking the parking lot every five seconds while fully checking the parking lot every five seconds. Maybe they're just running late. Maybe there's traffic. Maybe there's a *very large group* about to pull in all at once. Maybe they rented a party bus.

Nope. No one else came. Not one more car. Not one more woman. Just us.

I remember sitting there thinking, Wow. First big event, absolutely crushed it. Like do I cancel? Do we pivot? Do we just go shopping as a very exclusive two-person ministry experience?

But we stayed. We sat on those church steps and started talking. Real talk. Not small talk. Life talk. What she was walking through. What was heavy on her heart.

And then we prayed together. Right there. Just the two of us. No crowd. No event. No shopping caravan. Just one conversation. One moment. One life. And looking back, hindsight is everything. What I thought was a failure was actually exactly how God had planned it.

I had planned an event. God had planned an encounter.

Isn't that how it goes? We expect God to show up in the big moments. The packed rooms. The visible impact. The stories we can point to and say, "Look what happened." We expect glory to look obvious.

But Scripture tells a very different story. He didn't make an announcement in the Temple. He went to an unknown field. To a group of ordinary, overlooked, night-shift shepherds.

Read Luke 2:8-14. What do you notice about whom God chose to reveal Himself to first?

What is the message the angels proclaim?

Shepherds were not impressive people in that culture.[1]

They were socially overlooked by a lot of people.[2] It was a job that likely kept them ceremonially unclean because they were in constant contact with sheep giving birth to lambs and potentially dead animals out in the fields. Shepherds were also often viewed as untrustworthy because they would let their flocks graze on private property.

They were not anyone's first choice to be trustworthy messengers. Nor were they on anyone's top-ten list for getting a visit from heaven's angels. God showed up once again to the least expected audience around. They weren't trying to make a name for themselves. They were just there.

And that's where God met them. God was already shaking things up, from an unknown girl in Nazareth to an ordinary birth in Bethlehem. The shepherds were the next whisper from God that things were getting turned on

FAITH HABIT

Take a short walk and imagine what it felt like for the shepherds that night.

end. God was moving His glory from sacred spaces into everyday places. He was giving an open invitation to everyone rather than exclusive access to the elite.

The angels declare:

*"Glory to God in the highest heaven, and on earth peace."*

Glory is no longer distant. It has come to earth.

Read Luke 2:15-20. What do the shepherds do after encountering Jesus?

How do they respond to what they've seen?

These men were no longer just shepherds. They were evangelists. They were captivated. Their hearts and lives were moved in all the best ways. These shepherds became proclaimers. Their ordinary fields became a starting place for the Jesus movement to begin to grow to the ends of the earth.

Why does it seem like we are wired to always be waiting for something bigger? Or clearer? A different calling? A louder voice? A more important something?

What if God's invitation is closer?

- the conversation right in front of us
- the person God placed in our paths
- the moment that feels small but isn't

**God is not waiting for our lives to become impressive. He is already working in what is in front of us.**

God is not waiting for our lives to become impressive. He is already working in what is in front of us. Glory doesn't need a stage. It just needs a place to land. And maybe just maybe the reason our lives feel ordinary right now is not because God is absent, but because He is choosing that exact place to reveal His glory.

## CARRY THIS WITH YOU

*You Didn't Choose It. God Will Use It.*

Get your worship on with "Angels (Glory to God)" by Phil Wickham.

## LEARN IT. LIVE IT.

Fill in the blanks:

*"For my eyes have seen your ______________,*

*which you have ______________ in the sight of all ____________."*

*Luke 2:30-31*

# DAY 2: YOU DON'T NEED PERFECT WORDS

**Focus Verse**

*"For my eyes have seen your salvation,*
*which you have prepared in the sight of all nations."*
*Luke 2:30-31*

It was my senior year of high school, and I was sitting in English class at my very public school. We were in one of those debate units—maybe you know the kind. Big social issues. Big opinions. Big confidence from people who are seventeen and absolutely convinced they understand the world.

We had been breaking into groups, arguing different sides of things, and somehow the whole class got onto the topic of capital punishment. I don't remember exactly how we got there, but my teacher used it as an example and asked a question. She said something like, *"Is there anyone here who believes it is always wrong, in any circumstance, to take a life?"*

And I, without fully thinking it through, shot my hand straight up. Like immediate. Confident. Bold. And then I looked around. No one else's hand was up. Not one. Just me. Hanging out there. Alone. Spiritually confident for about 2.5 seconds.

And then immediately less confident. My teacher looked at me and said, *"Okay why?"* And I said, very theologically deep, very prepared, *"Uh . . . um . . . the Ten Commandments?" Pause. A little weaker, "Thou shalt not kill?"*[3]

And as soon as I said it, I had a full internal spiral: *"That is in there, right? That's a real commandment? Pretty sure that's legit. I think."*

Meanwhile, the class launched into debate mode. Scenarios. Exceptions. Arguments flying everywhere. And I just sat there thinking, *"I'm not sure I answered that right. Is that even what I believe? What just happened?"* Deep theological reflections from my seventeen-year-old brain.

Class ended, and I was ready to quietly disappear into the hallway and pretend none of that had ever happened. And then a girl walked up to me. She said, *"Hey, I just wanted to tell you that I really admired your courage to stand up for your faith like that."*

And I was like, *"Oh. Um . . . thanks."* Inside I'm thinking, *"Did I? Was that courage? Because it felt more like accidental participation."* But that moment stuck with me. Because what felt small, what felt awkward, what was completely unpolished and unplanned, God still used.

Please tell me you've had a moment like that. Anyone? We think sharing our faith has to be

- polished,
- confident,
- theologically airtight, and
- preferably not awkward.

We think we need the right words, the right moment, and just a little more clarity before we speak. But that's not what we see in Scripture. It's not about the words; it's about our attitude. First Peter 3:15 says, "Always be prepared to give an answer to everyone who asks you to give the reason for the hope that you have. But do this with gentleness and respect." The Bible's advice is to be gentle and respectful.

When the shepherds encountered Jesus, they didn't wait. They had angels in the night sky, a message from heaven, a star shining in the sky, and an epic hunt to find a baby.

**We think we need the right words, the right moment, and just a little more clarity before we speak. But that's not what we see in Scripture. It's not about the words; it's about our attitude.**

Read Luke 2:15-18. What do the shepherds decide to do after the angels leave?

What do they say after seeing Jesus?

Notice what Scripture does not say. It does not say

- they had everything figured out,
- they fully understood who Jesus was, or
- they carefully crafted a message.

FAITH HABIT

When someone asks about your weekend, mention church + what God taught you.

It simply says:

*"When they had seen him, they spread the word."*

They shared what they had seen. That's it. Not a thorough, perfect explanation. Just their story.

Read Acts 4:20 and 1 Peter 3:15-16.

This is the same pattern. What God does in you flows out of you.

At its core, sharing your faith is not about having all the answers. It's about sharing what you have seen God do. In the New Testament, the word witness (in the Greek *martyreō*) means "to testify" to what you have personally seen and experienced. The shepherds told what they had seen. And that is still how God works.

Read Luke 2:17-18 (again). What was the response of the people who heard the shepherds?

Scripture says they were amazed. Not because the shepherds were impressive, but because the message was. God was! So why don't we do the same? Why do we stay quiet? Maybe it's because

- we're afraid of getting it wrong,
- we don't feel "ready,"
- we don't want it to be awkward, or
- we think someone else could say it better.

Sound familiar? Because that's exactly where our stories live. You don't have to have a perfect answer. You don't have to have a prepared speech. Even if mid-sentence you are not sure if you're quoting Scripture correctly, God can still use it.

Where in your life do you feel hesitant to speak up about your faith?

What holds you back the most?

Who is one person in your life right now who might need to hear something true about God?

You just need a moment and a willingness to speak. The shepherds didn't have a script. They didn't have certainty. They didn't have credentials. They had a moment. And they took it.

Maybe when we feel a nudge in the middle of situations where we find ourselves completely unprepared, such as in the middle of a debate class on capital punishment, and aren't even sure what we think about the issue, remember that prompting from the Holy Spirit is not because you are ready but because someone else is.

CARRY THIS WITH YOU

*Don't Walk Away. Walk It Out.*

## LEARN IT. LIVE IT.

Fill in the blanks:

*"For my eyes have seen your ______________,*

*which you have ______________ in the sight of*

*all ____________."*

*Luke 2:30-31*

**Get your worship on with "Go On and Tell It" by Jeremy Camp.**

# DAY 3: DON'T MISS WHAT'S RIGHT IN FRONT OF YOU

**Focus Verse**

*"For my eyes have seen your salvation,*
*which you have prepared in the sight of all nations."*
*Luke 2:30-31*

When I was in seminary, I was living on a shoestring budget. Like a tight shoestring. I worked two jobs and helped manage the apartments I lived in just to help cover housing. Glamorous? No. Character building? Absolutely.

I lived in Pasadena for three years while I worked on my ministry degree, and, honestly, Pasadena is amazing. Diverse. Fun. Historical charm. A modern urban vibe. Any kind of ethnic food you could ever want. Approximately two thousand coffee shops (conservatively). Parks. Museums. The Rose Parade. It's a whole vibe.

But one thing I could not afford? A fancy salon. So when my friend told me about a place she went to called "Michell's," I was like, affordable hair? Yes, thank you, Lord. I called, and the guy answered the phone: "Michell's." Great. Confirmed. Locked in. Case closed.

So I started going regularly. It was a one-guy operation. Super simple. Super affordable. And honestly? He did a great job. I was thrilled. And I'm a talker. I love building relationships—especially with hair stylists. It's like a built-in hour of conversation. You sit down, and suddenly you're like, "So tell me about your childhood." So every time I went in, I was warm, friendly, and very consistent:

*"Hi, Michell!" "Thanks so much, Michell!" "See you next time, Michell!"*

For a year. A full year. Like seasons changed. Holidays came and went. And not once, not once, did he correct me. One day I ran into my friend Patty, the one who told me about the place. I was telling her how great Michell was and how grateful I was that she recommended him.

She looks at me, pauses, and says, "Lisa, his name is Philip."

I'm sorry.

Philip?

No.

No, it's not. I have receipts. I've been saying "Michell" for twelve months.

She said, "No. His name is Philip." I just stood there like, have I been confidently wrong for a year? Why did he never correct me? Was he just like, "You know what? Michell is who I am now. This is my new life." Did he go home and tell people, "I've been rebranded"? For an entire year I had been calling this man by the wrong name.

And here's the worst part: I thought I knew him. I had conversations with him. I sat in his chair regularly. We talked about life. I probably asked him deep questions. I may have prayed for him. And yet I didn't even know his name. I wasn't ignoring him. I just wasn't really paying attention. And it was also awkward. I think I just started calling him Philip after that and we never mentioned it.

It's amazing how easy it is to miss something important even when you're right in the middle of it. Sometimes we think we're paying attention but we're actually just familiar with what's right in front of us.

After Jesus is born, there are forty quiet days. Forty days of learning how to feed a newborn. Diapers. Swaddling. Trying to sleep. Forty days of healing from giving birth. Forty days of adjusting to a completely new life. Forty days where the miracle is real but mostly unseen.

According to the Law of Moses, after a woman gave birth, there was a period of purification.[4] This is what Mary would have followed.

Read Leviticus 12:1-4. What was required after the birth of a son?

For a baby boy, a mother would wait forty days before going to the Temple for purification and dedication. This wasn't punishment. It was a time to heal, to rest, and to prepare to re-enter the rhythms of worship in the community. So for forty days Mary and Joseph may have stayed in Bethlehem resting. Then after the established waiting period, they went to Jerusalem.

**Sometimes we think we're paying attention but we're actually just familiar with what's right in front of us.**

The Temple was in Jerusalem. This was the center of worship and sacrifice for the Jewish people. This was the place where God's presence dwelt in the Holy of Holies, which was the most sacred space in all of Israel.

Read Luke 2:22-24. Why did Mary and Joseph go to the Temple?

What offering did they bring?

They brought two doves or two young pigeons. This was the offering allowed for those who could not afford a lamb. Mary and Joseph—the parents of Jesus, the ones entrusted with the Son of God—were not wealthy.

And then there was another part of this moment. The dedication of the firstborn.

Read Exodus 13:2. What does God require of the firstborn?

Every firstborn son was to be set apart to the Lord. This practice went all the way back to the Exodus, to when God spared the firstborn of Israel. So every Jewish family would bring their firstborn son to the Temple as a declaration: This child belongs to God.

Read Luke 2:25-32. What do we learn about Simeon?

What had God promised him?

Simeon had been waiting. Not casually but faithfully. Intently. Expectantly. Scripture says the Holy Spirit was upon him. That he was looking for the consolation of Israel. He was watching. Waiting. Looking for God to move. And then one day Mary and Joseph walk in carrying a baby. Just another couple. Just another child. Just another ordinary moment in a very busy Temple. Except it wasn't. Simeon saw Him.

Not because Jesus looked different. Not because there was an announcement. Not because anyone else pointed Him out. But because the Holy Spirit had prepared Simeon's eyes to recognize what no one else could see. He takes Jesus in his arms and says, "My eyes have seen your salvation."

### FAITH HABIT

Ask God for help in one area where you feel weak today.

Read Luke 2:36-38. What do we learn about Anna?

What does she do when she sees Jesus?

Anna had also been waiting. Years. Decades. Worshipping. Fasting. Praying. And when she saw Jesus, she didn't hesitate. She recognized Him and began telling others. Anna was the first female evangelist!

Where in your life might God be present but you're missing it because it looks ordinary?

Worship with Katy Nicole and Matt Maher's "Our King Has Come."

God doesn't always reveal Himself in obvious ways. The question is not, "Is God here?" The question is, "Do you have eyes to see Him?"

CARRY THIS WITH YOU
*Let Go. Let God Lead.*

## LEARN IT. LIVE IT.

Fill in the blanks:

*"For my eyes have seen your ______________,*

*which you have ______________ in the sight of*

*all ____________."*

*Luke 2:30-31*

# DAY 4: IS IT WORTH IT? YES. YES, IT IS.

**Focus Verse**

*"For my eyes have seen your salvation,*
*which you have prepared in the sight of all nations."*
*Luke 2:30-31*

Ice cream is a big deal in my family. It is not a casual dessert situation. It's a lifestyle. A commitment. Possibly a spiritual discipline.

Every summer our family goes to Michigan to visit my mom and sisters—and all their families. It's a tradition that is filled with summer fun: boating, picnicking, celebrating the Fourth of July, and consuming what can only be described as medically questionable amounts of ice cream.

Now listen. If you've never had Ashby's Ice Cream, I need you to know you're missing out. This is not grocery-store ice cream. This is not "grab a tub and call it a day" ice cream. This is Michigan-level, small-town, creamy, dreamy, life-changing ice cream.

And for years, we had a system. A perfect system. There was a little ice cream shop just ten minutes from our house. Ten minutes! Practically in walking distance if we were motivated enough (we were not—but we liked knowing we could be).

And then tragedy. The shop closed. Just shut down. Lights off. Doors locked. Dreams crushed. We kept thinking, "Someone will buy it. Someone will reopen it. This cannot be the end of our story." But it just sat there. Empty. Mocking us. We had to face the harsh reality: Our ice cream glory days were over.

Until one day someone made a discovery. A holy discovery. A family-changing discovery. "Ashby's is at one of the gas stations." I'm sorry—what? Not a cute shop. Not a charming little downtown stop. A gas station. And not even our gas station. The one thirty minutes away.

And suddenly we had a decision to make. Are we really going to drive thirty minutes to a gas station for ice cream?

Yes.

Yes, we are.

And let me tell you, we did not hesitate. We loaded up the car like we were going on a mission. Because we were. A dairy-based mission. A creamy quest of greatness.

Find out more at ashbysicecream.com

And when we got there? Worth it. Completely worth it. It was unexpected. A little inconvenient. Slightly ridiculous. And absolutely worth the journey. Oh, and we got some gas too.

**There is something in us that will go out of our way for what we've decided is valuable.**

There is something in us that will go out of our way for what we've decided is valuable. We will drive farther. Wait longer. Spend more. Rearrange our plans. Not because we have to, but because we've decided: This is worth it.

After Jesus was born, God began drawing people to Him. We already saw it with the shepherds. But people were willing to seek Him out from even greater distances. In Matthew, we learn about another group of travelers who sought out Jesus. Mary must have been so shocked to have these men find them. Yet she also may have found it delightful to see another miraculous moment surrounding her son. A star leading them? Why not. God could do anything.

Read Matthew 2:1-2. Where do the wise men come from?

What are they looking for?

These wise men, often called *magi*, were scholars or likely astrologers from the East.[5] They studied the stars. They searched for meaning. They were looking for something greater than themselves. And then they saw something. A star. A star that was a sign beckoning them to make a journey. They didn't have a map or a plan, but they decided they must follow that star.

This wasn't a short trip for the Wise Guys. Depending on where they came from (and we don't know their exact location), this journey could have taken weeks or even months. These adventurous souls were determined to find out why that star was there. Some scholars believe they may have known the prophecy spoken by Balaam:

*"I see him, but not now;*
*I behold him, but not near.*
*A star will come out of Jacob;*
*a scepter will rise out of Israel."*
*Numbers 24:17*

Read Matthew 2:9-12. What happens when they finally find Jesus?

What do they do?

These men traveled a great distance and pursued Jesus. When the star stopped above Bethlehem and the wise men found Him there, they didn't hesitate; they bowed down and worshipped Him. The treasures they carried all those miles were opened and presented.

Gold. Frankincense. Myrrh.

These special gifts were meant to bestow honor and recognition on the new King.[6] They brought costly items to exalt Him above all others. The star led them for many miles. But ultimately the star led them to the One who would one day lead all who would believe.

## FAITH HABIT

Take the longer way home today and use the extra time to worship in your car.

**Worship with “We Three Kings” by Tommee Profitt.**

What would it look like in your life to pursue Jesus, not just when it’s easy, but when it costs you something?

You don’t pursue what you’re unsure about. You pursue what you’ve decided is worth it. The wise men didn’t just notice Jesus. They decided He was worth rearranging their lives for. Many believe that these costly gifts would help provide for the family as they would soon be forced to travel to protect Jesus.

Following Jesus will interrupt your plans. It will take more time than you expected. Cost more than you planned. Lead you further than you intended. And it will still be worth it. They didn’t have a full plan, just a star. And apparently, that’s all God needs.

**CARRY THIS WITH YOU**
*Strength Starts with Surrender.*

## LEARN IT. LIVE IT.

Fill in the blanks:

*“For my eyes have seen your ________________,*

*which you have _______________ in the sight of all ____________.”*

*Luke 2:30-31*

# DAY 5: YOU ARE NOT CARRYING THIS ALONE

**Focus Verse**

*"For my eyes have seen your salvation,*
*which you have prepared in the sight of all nations."*
*Luke 2:30-31*

When I was in college, I went on a mission trip to the Caribbean.

And before you say anything, yes, it was a real mission trip. Not a "sit on the beach and call it ministry" situation. We worked. Hard.

We were a performing arts team, which meant we had songs, dances, skits, and, yes, puppets. Nothing says "we're here to change lives" like a group of college students dramatically presenting the Gospel with puppets.

We traveled to schools, neighborhoods, and camps, sharing the hope of Jesus with kids and families. Some of the places we went were tough—areas with real need and real brokenness. We would set up our little performances, and while all the kids gathered in front of us, you could feel the adults watching from a distance. Leaning against fences. Standing in doorways. Sometimes dealing drugs. Pretending not to listen, but also listening.

It was equal parts beautiful and slightly terrifying. We stayed at a camp, cooked our own food, and traveled everywhere on a bus. And when I say "bus," I need you to adjust your mental image. This was not a vehicle. This was a faith exercise on wheels.

This bus was ancient. Like if buses had ancestry reports, this one would trace back to biblical times. I'm pretty sure Noah considered bringing it on the ark and then decided against it. It broke down. Constantly. Not occasionally. Not inconveniently. Constantly.

We would be driving along, minding our own business, and then suddenly, silence. The engine would just give up. Like, "I have done enough. I will go no further." And every single time, we all knew the drill. Everyone off the bus. We would climb out, line up behind it, and start pushing. A full team of sweaty, slightly confused college students pushing this giant bus down Caribbean roads.

We weren't just pushing. We were praying. Like full-on, hands-on-the-bus, "Lord Jesus, you did raise Lazarus from the dead, so we feel like this is within your skill set" kind of praying. I am convinced that bus ran more on prayer than gas. Honestly, I think angels just gave it a little nudge every time we needed to get somewhere. Because somehow, every time, we made it. We got to the schools. We got to the neighborhoods. I remember the pushing. The praying. And the way God kept showing up. Because we didn't carry the mission; God carried us.

Sometimes following God feels a lot like being on that bus. You're moving but not smoothly. You're going somewhere but not how you expected. Things break down. Plans change. You find yourself thinking: "Is this really how this is supposed to go?"

And that's exactly where Mary's story leads us. Because after the birth, after the shepherds, after the Temple, after the wise men. . . .

There's a part of the story that feels quieter. But it might be one of the most powerful. God didn't just bring Jesus into the world. He carried Him. He protected Him. He kept Him.

Read Matthew 2:13-15. What warning does Joseph receive?

Where does God tell them to go?

Right after the wise men leave, Joseph has a dream. An angel appears and says, "Get up, . . . take the child and his mother and escape to Egypt" (Matthew 2:13). Not later. Not when it's convenient. Not when he's a little older. Now. Because King Herod was searching for Jesus, and not to worship Him.

Herod the Great ruled under Roman authority and was known for both his power and his paranoia.[7] History tells us he was so threatened by potential rivals that he had members of his own family killed. So when he hears about a "new king," he doesn't celebrate; he tries to eliminate the threat. Matthew 2:16

tells us he horrifically ordered the killing of all boys two years old and under in Bethlehem.

This isn't just a sweet Christmas story anymore. This is dangerous. Urgent. Real. And right in the middle of it, God steps in. Joseph wakes up and takes action. He gets them moving. Immediately. No overthinking. No questioning. No delay. No backup plan. They had learned by now to trust God's directions even when they didn't make sense. They were leaving the country with no passports. They didn't know when or if they were coming back. But they trusted God's guidance and protection better than witness protection.

Mary once again was on the road. From Nazareth to the Judean Hill Country and back to Nazareth. From Nazareth to Bethlehem. From Bethlehem to Jerusalem. And now to Egypt. She was definitely getting her steps in.

We don't know how long the family stayed in Egypt. Scholars believe the range was anywhere from a few months to a few years, until after King Herod died in 4 BCE.

But Egypt was part of God's plan all along. The prophet Hosea wrote in Hosea 11:1, "Out of Egypt I called my son," and his prophecy finds fulfillment as Jesus is called out of Egypt to return to Israel.[8]

Read Matthew 2:19-23. What happens after Herod dies?

Where does the family eventually settle?

After some time in Egypt, God speaks again: "Go back." And once again Joseph, Mary, and Jesus move back to Nazareth. And that's where Jesus grows up. Ordinary. Protected. Carried. Kept.

**God is willing and able to carry each of us.**

God carried this story to us. He kept His promises. God is still doing that today. He is willing and able to carry each of us.

### FAITH HABIT

Lift a weight (or a can), name what's heavy, say "God is carrying this," and then set it down.

Read Isaiah 46:4:

*"I have made you and I will carry you;*
*I will sustain you and I will rescue you."*

That's not just true for Jesus. That's true for you.

Where in your life do you feel like you are pushing a broken-down bus right now? Where do you need God's strength?

**You were never meant to carry your life on your own. God doesn't just call you; He carries you. God doesn't just send you; He sustains you.**

Because here's the truth: You were never meant to carry your life on your own. God doesn't just call you; He carries you. God doesn't just send you; He sustains you.

**This is the strength to carry.**

Not strength that comes from you. Strength that comes from God.

Not strength that removes the weight. Strength that meets you in it.

Not strength that makes life easy. Strength that makes you steady.

The truth is that you don't have the strength to carry everything in your life. But you were never supposed to. God does.

This is what Mary learned. This is what Joseph lived. This is what this entire story has been showing us all along.

**The strength to carry was never meant to come from you.**

It comes from God.

Read 2 Corinthians 12:9. How does God's power help us in our weakness?

Not a strength that removes the weight but a strength that meets you in it. Not a strength that makes life easy but a strength that makes you steady.

You are carrying things you didn't choose. Responsibilities. Heartaches. Unanswered questions. A story that doesn't always look the way you thought it would.

But you are not carrying them alone.

The same God who carried Mary is carrying you.

The same God who protected Jesus is protecting you.

The same God who guided every step is guiding yours.

He will not drop what He has chosen to hold.

So when life feels heavy, remember:

You are not just carrying your life; you are being carried by God.

And He always gives you . . . **the strength to carry.**

> CARRY THIS WITH YOU
>
> *If He Called You to It, He'll Carry You Through It.*

## LEARN IT. LIVE IT.

Fill in the blanks:

*"For my eyes have seen your _______________,*

*which you have _______________ in the sight of*

*all ____________."*

*Luke 2:30-31*

Get your worship on with Chris Tomlin with CeCe Winans and sing "O Holy Night."

# VIDEO VIEWER GUIDE: WEEK 4

Sometimes faith begins with a "yes" we don't fully ______________.

The quiet night of Bethlehem became the loudest ______________ in heaven.

Good news always moves people __________ Jesus.

The Shepherd of our ________ was born in a place meant for sheep.

Faith is trusting God in the life you didn't _________.

God gives us the ____________ to carry the life we didn't choose.

The God who calls us walks ______ us.

The same God who sustained Mary is the God who ____________ us.

# DISCUSSION QUESTIONS: WEEK 4

- Lisa shared the sweet story of her son saying "tree" and how it made something familiar feel full of wonder again. What is something familiar in Christmas or in everyday life that still has the power to fill you with wonder?

- The shepherds were ordinary people working an ordinary night when heaven suddenly broke in. What stands out to you most about God choosing shepherds to be the first to hear the news of Jesus's birth?

- Luke says Mary "treasured up all these things and pondered them in her heart." What do you think it looks like in real life to slow down, treasure what God is doing, and reflect instead of rushing past it?

- This talk highlights Jesus as both the Good Shepherd and the Lamb of God. How does seeing Jesus in both of those roles deepen your understanding of who He is and what He came to do?

- Lisa said, "Faith is trusting God in the life you didn't choose." Where in your life right now do you most need to remember that the God who calls you is also the God who sustains you?

- Looking back over Mary's story, what part of her journey encourages you most in your own journey right now? What will you remember most about her in this study?

# A Final Word

There were many moments in my life when I did not understand what God was doing. The night the angel appeared, I did not understand why God would choose a young girl from Nazareth to carry His promise. When Joseph and I traveled the long road to Bethlehem, I did not understand why the Savior of the world would be born in a place meant for animals. And in the years that followed, there were many moments when the path before us felt uncertain.

But I learned something as I walked with God through each of those moments. God does not always show us the whole road ahead. Sometimes, He simply places the next step before us and asks us to trust Him.

When Gabriel first spoke to me, I had a choice. I could cling to the life I thought I wanted, or I could trust the God who was inviting me into something greater than I could imagine. I chose to trust Him. Not because I understood everything, but because I believed that the God who calls us is faithful to carry us.

When Gabriel first spoke to me, I believed I was being asked to carry something fragile. A promise. A calling. A child.

But over time, I came to understand something deeper. I was never carrying this story alone. The God who placed this child in my arms was the same God who held me in His hands.

When the road was long, He sustained me. When fear crept in, He steadied me. When I did not know what to do next, He led me. He carried me. And He kept me.

# From Mary

You may find yourself in a season you did not expect. A road you did not plan. A story that feels heavier than anything you ever imagined carrying. But I want you to remember something that I learned on my journey.

The God who asks you to hold something difficult will also give you the strength to carry it. Not a strength that comes from you, but a strength that comes from God.

The same God who was faithful in my life will be faithful in yours.

So when the road feels uncertain, when the weight feels heavy, whisper the prayer that once fell from my own trembling lips:

> "I am the Lord's servant. . . . May your word to me be fulfilled."
>
> Luke 1:38

The God who carried me is carrying you. He will never leave you to carry your story alone.

# VIDEO VIEWER GUIDE: ANSWERS

## INTRODUCTION

noticed

routine

anticipation

strength

## WEEK 1

invitations

Trust

stronger

clarity

already

## WEEK 2

confirmation

people

Elizabeth

character

powerful

character

## WEEK 3

yes

obedience

calling

steady

exactly

quiet

ordinary

courage

faithfulness

step

steady

## WEEK 4

understand

celebration

toward

souls

choose

strength

with

sustains

LEADER GUIDE

# INTRODUCTION

Many of us are walking roads we didn't plan to be on—carrying responsibilities we didn't choose, navigating disappointments we didn't see coming, or facing circumstances that feel heavier than we imagined we could bear. In those moments, it's easy to wonder where God is and whether we have what it takes to keep going.

But Scripture reminds us that God often does His most powerful work in the middle of the unexpected.

In *The Strength to Carry: Faith for the Life You Didn't Choose*, we step into one of the most familiar yet deeply profound stories in the Bible, the arrival of Jesus, and we see it through the eyes of Mary. Her ordinary life was interrupted by an extraordinary calling that required courage, surrender, and unwavering trust in God.

Mary's story matters to us because it reflects our own. Like her, we are often called to walk forward without knowing all the details. Like her, we are invited to trust God in the unknown. And like her, we discover that God does not leave us to carry what He places in our hands on our own.

Over the course of this four-week study, participants will

- discover how God meets us in unexpected seasons,
- learn to trust Him when the future feels uncertain,
- experience His strength in the midst of life's burdens, and
- embrace the hope of Emmanuel—God with us—in every moment.

As we walk through the story of Jesus's birth, we will see that it is more than a beautiful Christmas narrative; it's a powerful declaration that God has stepped into our world and continues to walk with us today. And as we follow Mary's journey, we will be reminded that the same God who strengthened her is faithful to strengthen us.

## ABOUT THIS LEADER GUIDE

As you gather each week with your group, you have the opportunity to create a space where women can connect with one another and encounter God through His Word.

Together, you will watch the teaching videos (if you choose to), engage in meaningful discussion, and encourage one another in faith.

This leader guide and the video teachings are your primary tools for leading your group through this study. Each session is designed to help participants reflect on what they are learning and apply it to their everyday lives.

You might choose to follow a format similar to one of these:

**60-Minute Format**

- Welcome/Opening Prayer (3–5 minutes)
- Icebreaker (5 minutes)
- Video Teaching (10–15 minutes)
- Group Discussion (30 minutes)
- Prayer Requests (5–10 minutes)

**90-Minute Format**

- Welcome/Opening Prayer (5–8 minutes)
- Icebreaker (5 minutes)
- Video Teaching (10–15 minutes)
- Group Discussion (40 minutes)
- Extended Conversation or Activity (10–15 minutes)
- Prayer Requests (10–15 minutes)

Each gathering includes the same core elements: connection, discussion, and prayer. Feel free to adapt to meet the needs of your group. For example, note that you likely won't have time to get to all of the discussion questions for a given session. That's okay! Start with the one or two you think will generate the richest conversation for your particular group. Also, although prayers are provided for each session, please feel free to modify them or disregard them; they are meant to be helpful, not prescriptive.

Encourage participants to complete each week's daily readings on their own before each group meeting. Each day includes stories and teaching from Lisa Toney, Scripture reading, reflection questions, and practical ways to apply God's word. However, remind your group that the goal is not perfection but connection with Jesus.

Remind participants that it's okay to adapt the study as needed. Some days may be difficult or busy, especially during the Christmas season. Simply spending time in God's word—whether it's early in the morning, during a lunch break, or in a quiet moment at the end of the day—is enough to stay engaged.

If your group includes women who are new to Bible study, offer reassurance and encouragement. This is a no-pressure, no-experience-required place to learn, explore, and grow together.

Finally, encourage connection beyond the pages of the study. Life is better when we walk alongside one another. Weekly gatherings provide not only accountability but also an opportunity to build meaningful relationships rooted in faith.

As you begin this journey together, trust that God will show up in powerful and unexpected ways, as He did for Mary so long ago.

# LEADER HELPS

## PREPARING FOR THE SESSIONS

- Prepare your meeting space before each group session. If you're meeting in person, do you have enough chairs? If you're meeting virtually, does everyone have the link they need?
- Pray for your group and each group member by name. Ask God to work in the life of every woman in your group.
- Review the week's readings and the session outline in this leader guide. If it's helpful, mark the discussion questions you know you'll want to cover and make notes about anything you know you want to share during discussion time.

## LEADING THE SESSIONS

- Personally greet each woman as she arrives. If desired, take attendance using your group roster. (This will assist you in identifying members who have missed several sessions so that you may contact them and let them know they were missed.)
- At the start of each session, ask the women to turn off or silence their cell phones.
- Encourage everyone to participate fully, but don't put anyone on the spot. Be prepared to offer a personal example or answer if no one else responds at first.
- Facilitate but don't dominate. Remember that if you talk most of the time, group members may tend to listen passively rather than to engage personally.
- Try not to interrupt, judge, or minimize anyone's comments or input.
- Remember that you are not expected to be the expert or have all the answers. Acknowledge that all of you are on this journey together, with the Holy Spirit as your leader and guide. If issues or questions arise that you don't feel equipped to answer or handle, talk with the pastor or a staff member at your church.

- Encourage good discussion, but don't be timid about calling time on a particular question and moving ahead. Part of your responsibility is to keep the group on track.
- Try to end on time. If you are running over, give members the opportunity to leave if they need to. Then wrap up as quickly as you can.
- Be prepared for some women to want to hang out and talk at the end. If you need everyone to leave by a certain time, communicate this at the beginning of the session. If you are meeting in a church during regularly scheduled activities or have arranged for childcare, be sensitive to the agreed-upon ending time.
- Thank the women for coming and let them know you're looking forward to seeing them next time.

# SESSION OUTLINES

## WEEK 1: THE PATH YOU DIDN'T CHOOSE

### FOCUS VERSE

*"For no word from God will ever fail."*
*Luke 1:37*

### OPENING PRAYER

*God with us, thank You for bringing us together to set aside some time in this busy season to dwell in Your unfailing Word. We ask You to help us keep our minds open to what You have to say to us today and our hearts willing to respond to what we hear. We pray all this in the name of Jesus, Your Word made flesh, the ultimate Christmas gift. Amen.*

### ICEBREAKER

Invite participants to briefly answer this icebreaker question:

- What's one small, "everyday" moment from this past week that, looking back, meant more to you than you expected?

### VIDEO DISCUSSION

You may choose to watch both the introduction video and the week 1 video during your first meeting, or you might send the intro video to participants ahead of time. As needed, use the questions below to guide discussion and get participants talking.

#### Intro Video

- It feels appropriate to open our time together with childhood Christmas memories like the one Lisa shares. What's one Christmas memory from your childhood that still makes you smile?

- As a child, Lisa reached for her sister's hand when she felt afraid. Who or what do you instinctively reach for when life feels overwhelming?
- This video contrasts the wonder of Christmas with the busyness of the season. Where do you feel that tension most in your life right now? What helps you slow down and notice God during busy seasons?

### Week 1 Video

- The story begins with a completely normal lunch that suddenly turns into an emergency. Have you ever had a day that shifted unexpectedly like that—something small that turned into a big moment?
- Lisa says, "Trust begins where control ends." What does that idea stir up in you?
- Mary's "yes" led to a meaningful life, but not an easy one. How do you wrestle with the tension between wanting an easy life versus a purposeful one?
- The video ends with the idea that God is already present in the interruption and He gives us strength to carry what He asks. Where do you need to believe that right now?

## GROUP DISCUSSION

These questions also appear in the participant workbook portion of the book. The goal is to give group participants questions about which they can think and prepare to speak on before group meetings. You can choose to use as many or as few questions as make sense for your group time.

### Introduction

- Share your name and the people and the animals you live with.
- Where do you spend your time most days of the week?
- What is one of your favorite things about Christmas?
- What do you like to do for fun?
- Share your "why" for being part of this study. What are you hoping the Lord will do through this in your life?

### Week 1

- What's a small moment in your life that suddenly took an unexpected turn like Lisa's sesame seed story?
- When you picture Mary living her ordinary life in Nazareth before the angel appeared, what stands out to you about the way God chose to begin this story?
- Can you think of a time when your plans were suddenly interrupted or redirected? What emotions did you feel in that moment?
- Lisa said, "Interruptions are often invitations." What do you think God might invite us to in seasons when life doesn't go according to plan?
- Mary responded to the angel by saying, "I am the Lord's servant." What do you think helped her trust God enough to say "yes" in such an uncertain moment?
- What do you need to trust God with this week?

## BOOK DISCUSSION

### Week 1, Day 1: Just Another Tuesday Until God Shows Up

*Carry This with You:*

Ordinary You. Extraordinary God.

*Discussion Questions*

- Our focus verse says, "For no word from God will ever fail." Where do you find that hardest to trust in your current season, especially in the "ordinary" parts of life?
- Lisa says God isn't looking for impressive people but for willing hearts. What do you think "willingness" looks like in real, everyday life?
- Lisa uses Mary's example to suggest that God prepares us in ordinary seasons. Looking back, can you identify a time when God was shaping or preparing you before something significant? What did you learn from that season?

### Week 1, Day 2: When God Messes with Your Plans

*Carry This with You:*

Didn't See It Coming. God Did.

*Discussion Questions*

- Think about Lisa's story about the unexpected scholarship. Have you ever received a "no" that later turned into something different? What did that experience teach you about trusting God's timing?
- The devotional suggests that interruptions can be invitations from God. How do you personally discern the difference between a distraction and a divine redirection?
- Isaiah 55:8-9 reminds us that God's ways are higher than ours. Why do you think God's interruptions often feel confusing or even frustrating at first? How can we grow in trusting Him in those moments?

## Week 1, Day 3: The Kind of "Yes" That Changes Everything

*Carry This with You*

Surrender First. Understand Later.

*Discussion Questions*

- Lisa highlights the difference between a casual "yep" and a committed "yes." Where in your life might you be giving God a half-hearted response instead of a fully surrendered one?
- Mary's "yes" was courageous and costly. What fears or concerns tend to hold you back from fully obeying God when He nudges you?
- Look at the verses about obedience (James 1:22; Luke 11:28; Hebrews 11:8; John 14:15; 1 Samuel 15:22; Deuteronomy 5:33). Which one stands out most to you, and how could you live it out in a practical way this week?

## Week 1, Day 4: Stop Spiraling. Start Holding.

*Carry This with You*

Hold the Word. Drop the Worry.

*Discussion Questions*

- Today's devotional opens with those late-night "mental replays." What's something small or funny your brain tends to fixate on when you're trying to fall asleep?

- Lisa talks about the difference between replaying and holding. How do you personally recognize when you've crossed from healthy reflection into unhealthy spiraling?
- We can choose to return to what is true instead of what we don't understand. What truths about God do you need to come back to in this season—and why those in particular?

### Week 1, Day 5: That-a-Girl. Walk. It. Out.

*Carry This with You:* Keep Walking. God's Working.

*Discussion Questions*

- Where in your life do you feel "stuck" right now? What do you think might be holding you there?
- Mary relies on both movement and community in this next step. Who are the people you can "walk with" in your faith right now, and how do they help you keep going?
- The "Carry This with You" phrase for today is "Keep Walking. God's Working." How might your mindset shift if you truly believed God was working in the middle of your slow or uncertain progress?

## PRAYER REQUESTS

## CLOSING PRAYER

*God, we lift up to You the prayer requests we've heard spoken out loud and those too weighty to share right now. We trust that You know about all of them and that You are working in each of us. Thank You for this time together, and we ask You to help us walk courageously along the paths You have for us in the coming week. Amen.*

# WEEK 2: BELIEVING BIG PROMISES

## FOCUS VERSE

*"Blessed is she who has believed that the Lord would fulfill his promises to her!"*
*Luke 1:45*

## OPENING PRAYER

*God who gives us each other, we thank You for the chance to be together today. We bring our excitement for this joyous season, and we bring our disappointments and unmet expectations, and we trust You to help us carry all of it. May our ears be open to hear from You and from our sisters. Amen.*

## ICEBREAKER

Invite participants to briefly answer this icebreaker question:

- What is your favorite Christmas song, and why?

## VIDEO DISCUSSION

As needed, use the questions below to guide discussion and get participants talking.

### Week 2 Video

- This week's video highlights how God often sends people (like Elizabeth) to strengthen us. Who has been an "Elizabeth" in your life? How did they encourage or support you?
- On the flip side, when have you had the opportunity to be an "Elizabeth" for someone else?
- Lisa's phrase "what we magnify determines what feels powerful" is a key idea this week. What are you currently "magnifying" in your life? How is it affecting your peace or perspective?

## GROUP DISCUSSION

- Lisa shared about switching from a real Christmas tree to an artificial one. What is a small tradition or expectation you had growing up that didn't turn out quite the way you imagined in adulthood?

- Have you ever had a season where you felt like you were carrying something heavy or unexpected—like the backpack Lisa described? What made that season challenging?
- Mary was strengthened when Elizabeth recognized what God was doing in her life. Has there ever been someone who encouraged or confirmed God's work in your life during a difficult season?
- Mary responded by worshipping and magnifying God in the Magnificat. Why do you think focusing on God's character can strengthen us when our circumstances feel overwhelming?
- Where might God be inviting you this week to either receive encouragement—or be an "Elizabeth" for someone else who needs strength?
- What is one thing you are carrying right now that you could intentionally bring to God in prayer this week?

## BOOK DISCUSSION

### Week 2, Day 1: God Saw You Before You Saw It

*Carry This with You*
God's Already There.

*Discussion Questions*

- Lisa shares about missing the opportunity to connect with someone nearby. Have you ever realized after the fact that God had placed something or someone in your life that you didn't fully recognize at the time? What did you learn from that?
- Elizabeth and Zechariah lived with long-term disappointment while remaining faithful. How have you seen disappointment shape your faith, either positively or negatively?
- Waiting seasons can make us question God's timing or goodness. What is something you are currently waiting on or wrestling with? How is that affecting your trust in God?

### Week 2, Day 2: While You Were Waiting, God Was Working

*Carry This with You*
Delay Is Not Denial.

*Discussion Questions*

- The phrase "God's silence is not His absence; it is often His preparation" is central to today's study. How does that perspective challenge or comfort you?
- Elizabeth responds to Mary with immediate faith and affirmation, not skepticism. Why do you think it can sometimes be difficult to celebrate or rejoice in what God is doing in someone else's life? What helps you move toward encouragement?
- Elizabeth had to release her expectations of how her life would turn out before she ever saw God move. What is something you may need to release—an expectation, a timeline, an outcome—to start to trust God more fully in this season?

## Week 2, Day 3: You're Not Crazy—God Said That

*Carry This with You*

If God Said It, He'll Confirm It.

*Discussion Questions*

- Mary "hurried" to Elizabeth after receiving the angel's message. What does that tell you about how Mary responded to God's direction? How do you typically respond when you sense God leading you?
- Lisa asks us to consider the voices we're listening to. Who are the primary voices influencing you right now? Are they strengthening your faith or feeding fear? What might need to change?
- God used Elizabeth to confirm what He had already spoken to Mary. Is there something you believe God has placed on your heart that you're still seeking confirmation for? What would it look like to remain open to how He might affirm it?

## Week 2, Day 4: When Gratitude Sneaks Up on You

*Carry This with You*

His Promise. My Peace.

*Discussion Questions*

- Lisa shares how God provided help in an unexpected and abundant way. Can you think of a time when God met a need in your life not just adequately but generously?
- Today's study highlights that worship often flows from recognizing God's goodness. Where have you seen evidence of God's kindness or faithfulness recently, even in small ways?
- Mary didn't wait for clarity before she praised; she trusted God in the middle of the unknown. What would it look like for you to choose worship before things make sense in an area of your life?

### Week 2, Day 5: Back to Real Life (but Different)

*Carry This with You*

What God Begins, He Completes.

*Discussion Questions*

- Mary experienced a meaningful, faith-filled season with Elizabeth. Then she had to return to real life. Have you ever had a "mountaintop" or spiritually rich season that eventually ended? What was it like to transition back into everyday life?
- Mary didn't have all the answers, but she kept moving forward anyway. What is one step of obedience you can sense God inviting you to take, even if you don't feel fully ready?
- Mary's story reminds us that God is often working not just in us but in the people around us, even when we can't see it. Is there a situation or relationship in your life where you need to trust that God is working behind the scenes? What makes that difficult?

## PRAYER REQUESTS

## CLOSING PRAYER

*God, we lift up to You the prayer requests we've heard spoken out loud and those too weighty to share right now. We trust that You know about all of them and that You are working in each of us. Thank You for this time together, and we ask You to keep our eyes open to chances to walk alongside others who need to share the weight of their burdens in the week ahead. Amen.*

# WEEK 3: GLORY AND PEACE

## FOCUS VERSE

*"Glory to God in the highest heaven,*
*and on earth peace to those on whom his favor rests."*
*Luke 2:14*

## OPENING PRAYER

*God of glory, thank You for bringing us together again to share some time in Your presence. We bring our confusion and questions and desire for control, and we ask You to help us lay all of it at Your feet and trust that You are making a way for us, just as You did for Mary and Joseph. Prepare our hearts for joyful obedience. Amen.*

## ICEBREAKER

Invite participants to briefly answer this icebreaker question:

- Are you more of a detailed planner or someone who takes life as it comes? How do you usually respond when plans suddenly change?

## VIDEO DISCUSSION

As needed, use the questions below to guide discussion and get participants talking.

### Week 3 Video

- The idea that "faith looks like a long walk of obedience" is central to this week's video. What helps you keep going when obedience feels slow, inconvenient, or difficult?
- Lisa reminds us that God often works in ordinary, unseen moments. Where in your life does faithfulness feel unnoticed or ordinary right now? How does it encourage you to know God sees it and is present in it?
- "God rarely reveals the whole plan; He usually reveals the next step." Why is it so hard to trust God with just the next step? What would it look like for you to live that way this week?

## GROUP DISCUSSION

- Lisa described the crowded, chaotic experience of Bethlehem during the Journey to Bethlehem event. Have you ever been part of a big event, trip, or holiday that didn't feel calm or peaceful at all—but was still memorable? What made it memorable?
- Mary and Joseph traveled about ninety miles to Bethlehem, likely walking many days in simple sandals. What part of Mary and Joseph's journey to Bethlehem stands out to you the most when you imagine what that trip might have been like?
- Lisa said, "Faith sometimes looks less like a moment . . . and more like a long walk of obedience." Can you think of a season in your life where faith felt more like a long journey than a single decision?
- Mary had already said yes to God, but life didn't suddenly become easier. Why do you think it can be difficult to keep trusting God when obedience leads to inconvenience or uncertainty?
- Luke says Mary "treasured up all these things and pondered them in her heart." What do you think it looks like in real life to remain steady in faith when circumstances feel chaotic or unclear?
- Lisa ended by asking the question: "Lord, what is the next faithful step you want me to take today?" What might be one "next faithful step" God could be inviting you to take in this season of your life?

## BOOK DISCUSSION

### Week 3, Day 1: When Nothing Makes Sense but God Is Working

*Carry This with You*

Unexpected Doesn't Mean Unplanned.

*Discussion Questions*

- Lisa shares about a time when what felt like rejection in her life turned out to be redirection. Can you think of a time when something didn't work out the way you wanted, but later you saw God's hand in it?

- Joseph chose restraint and quiet integrity instead of reacting out of hurt or self-protection. Why do you think it can be so difficult to respond with that kind of quiet strength when we feel wronged or confused?
- We often associate strength with confidence and control, but today's study reframes strength as trust and surrender. What does "strength" look like in your life right now? Has your definition of strength been challenged in any way?

### Week 3, Day 2: When God Finally Speaks

*Carry This with You*

God Will Make a Way Through This.

*Discussion Questions*

- The angel's first words were "Do not be afraid." Why do you think God so often addresses fear before anything else? What does that reveal about His heart toward us?
- Lisa emphasizes that God's Word anchors us even when it doesn't answer every question. Can you share a time when Scripture grounded you during a difficult or unclear season?
- Joseph went to sleep in confusion and woke up with direction, but he still had to act on it. Is there an area of your life where you sense God has already given you enough clarity for the next step, but you're hesitant to move forward? Why?

### Week 3, Day 3: You Don't Have to Do This Alone

*Carry This with You*

Follow God Now. He'll Explain Later.

*Discussion Questions*

- Joseph's obedience wasn't just internal; it became public and costly. Where in your life might God be inviting you to move from private belief to visible obedience?
- Lisa reminds us that Joseph's strength wasn't just for him but also directly impacted Mary and Jesus. How have you seen your own obedience (or someone else's) affect others in ways you didn't expect?

- Reflect on a time when someone "stood with you" rather than fixing everything. What did their presence provide that solutions could not?

### Week 3, Day 4: This Is Not How I Planned It

*Carry This with You*

Hope Has a Name.

*Discussion Questions*

- The entrance to the Church of the Nativity requires people to physically bow. What does "bowing" (humility and surrender) look like in your life right now?
- Mary's journey required physical endurance, emotional trust, and spiritual surrender all at once. Which of those feels most challenging for you in this season?
- The "Carry This with You" statement for today is "Hope Has a Name." When life feels uncertain or disrupted, what does it practically look like to anchor your hope in Jesus rather than in plans or outcomes?

### Week 3, Day 5: Well, That Wasn't What I Expected

*Carry This with You*

Awe Leads to Action.

*Discussion Questions*

- Jesus's birth didn't align with anyone's expectations of how a king should arrive. How do your expectations of how God should work sometimes shape or limit your ability to recognize what He's doing?
- Mary experienced the fulfillment of God's promise in a setting that felt ordinary and even uncomfortable. Where in your life might God be present, but it's hard to see because the circumstances don't feel "significant" enough?
- The name "Jesus" means "the Lord saves," and "Emmanuel" means "God with us." Which of those truths do you find yourself needing more right now: God as Savior or God as present with you? Why?

## PRAYER REQUESTS

## CLOSING PRAYER

*God, we lift up to You the prayer requests we've heard spoken out loud and those too weighty to share right now. We trust that You know about all of them and that You are working in each of us. Thank You for this time together, and we ask You to keep our eyes open to awe and our hearts open to hope this week. Amen.*

# WEEK 4: KEEP YOUR EYES OPEN

## FOCUS VERSE

*"For my eyes have seen your salvation,*
*which you have prepared in the sight of all nations."*
*Luke 2:30-31*

## OPENING PRAYER

*God of goodness, thank You for one more opportunity to be together to treasure and ponder the truth of the Christmas story. We celebrate all You have done in our lives, and we anticipate all You have yet to do in and through us. Give us eyes to see Your salvation and ears to hear Your good news during our time together today. Amen.*

## ICEBREAKER

Invite participants to briefly answer this icebreaker question:

- Lisa says that good news always moves people toward Jesus. What's one recent piece of good news, big or small, you can share with the group to help us move toward Jesus together in our last session?

## VIDEO DISCUSSION

As needed, use the questions below to guide discussion and get participants talking.

### Week 4 Video

- The shepherds didn't hesitate; they went to see Jesus right away. What does it look like in your life to "move toward Jesus" when you sense God is at work? What tends to hold you back?
- The shepherds responded to awe with action: They went, they told, they praised. Where might God be inviting you to move from awareness to action in your faith right now?
- Mary "treasured and pondered" what was happening rather than rushing past it. What practices help you slow down enough to recognize and reflect on what God is doing in your life?

## GROUP DISCUSSION

- Lisa shared the sweet story of her son saying "tree" and how it made something familiar feel full of wonder again. What is something familiar in Christmas or in everyday life that still has the power to fill you with wonder?
- The shepherds were ordinary people working an ordinary night when heaven suddenly broke in. What stands out to you most about God choosing shepherds to be the first to hear the news of Jesus's birth?
- Luke says Mary "treasured up all these things and pondered them in her heart." What do you think it looks like in real life to slow down, treasure what God is doing, and reflect instead of rushing past it?
- This talk highlights Jesus as both the Good Shepherd and the Lamb of God. How does seeing Jesus in both of those roles deepen your understanding of who He is and what He came to do?
- Lisa said, "Faith is trusting God in the life you didn't choose." Where in your life right now do you most need to remember that the God who calls you is also the God who sustains you?
- Looking back over Mary's story, what part of her journey encourages you most in your own journey right now? What will you remember most about her in this study?

## BOOK DISCUSSION

### Week 4, Day 1: Don't Miss It: God Is Right Here

*Carry This with You*

You Didn't Choose It. God Will Use It.

*Discussion Questions*

- Have you ever planned an event or outing and been disappointed with the response to it, like in Lisa's story from today? Looking back, what good do you see in that?
- Lisa turned her disappointment over a big event into an opportunity for an intimate moment of connection. Where might God be inviting you to simplify so you can connect with Him or someone He's put in your life?

- By sending angels to ordinary shepherds to announce the birth of Jesus in a nearby cave, God moved His glory "from sacred spaces into everyday places." What do you typically picture when you think of God's glory? Where might you look to find it in your life today?

### Week 4, Day 2: You Don't Need Perfect Words

*Carry This with You*

Don't Walk Away; Walk It Out.

*Discussion Questions*

- In Luke 2, the shepherds don't pause to process or discuss among themselves before they act. What stands out to you about their immediate response?
- Which of this session's reasons for not speaking up (fear of getting it wrong, not feeling ready, avoiding awkwardness, thinking someone else could do better) do you most relate to? Why do you think that holds you back?
- What is one simple, honest thing you can say about what God has done in your life?

### Week 4, Day 3: Don't Miss What's Right in Front of You

*Carry This with You*

Let Go. Let God Lead.

*Discussion Questions*

- Have you ever found out you've been wrong about a fact or detail for a long time, either something silly like Lisa's hair stylist example or something more substantial? How did you respond?
- Was there a time in your life when you felt like you'd been waiting forever for a sign from God or for something to happen, and it finally did? How did you respond to recognizing God?
- Lisa writes that the question isn't whether God is here but whether we have eyes to see Him. What practices or habits do you use as you're looking for God in your everyday life?

### Week 4, Day 4: Is It Worth It? Yes. Yes, It Is.

*Carry This with You*

Strength Starts with Surrender.

*Discussion Questions*

- What is something you or your family deem valuable enough to go out of your way or inconvenience yourself for? What makes it worth it?
- Has there ever been a time in your life when following Jesus cost you something? What happened?
- The wise men in today's session are the latest examples of characters who had to literally go on a journey to fulfill their part of the Christmas story. What stands out to you about the multiple travel stories from this Advent study (Mary to Elizabeth and back home, Mary and Joseph to Bethlehem, the wise men to Bethlehem)?

### Week 4, Day 5: You Are Not Carrying This Alone

*Carry This with You*

If He Called You to It, He'll Carry You Through It.

*Discussion Questions*

- Lisa describes moments on a mission trip when the only option was to stop, push, and pray. Where in your life right now do you feel like you're "pushing a broken-down bus"?
- Isaiah 46:4 says God will carry, sustain, and rescue His people. Which of those three words do you most need to hear right now? What makes that one stand out?
- Our final "Carry This with You" phrase is "If He called You to It, He'll Carry You Through It." Where do you need to stop trying to carry something alone? What would it look like this week to actually trust God (and maybe some of your friends from this study) with the weight you've been holding?

## WRAP-UP DISCUSSION

- If it's helpful and as time allows, you might end your time together with some general discussion looking back on the study as a whole.

- What day or week of *The Strength to Carry* most resonated with you?
- Which character we discussed—Mary, Elizabeth, Zechariah, Joseph, the shepherds, or someone else—do you most relate with at this point in your life? Which character do you most hope to become more like?
- What is one piece of encouragement, advice, or wisdom someone shared during our time together that you'll carry with you?

## PRAYER REQUESTS

## CLOSING PRAYER

*God, we lift up to You the prayer requests we've heard spoken out loud and those too weighty to share right now. We trust that You know about all of them and that You are working in each of us. Thank You for the gift of these past weeks together, for the courage and vulnerability to share our lives with one another, and for the strength and faithfulness to carry one another. We ask You to help us remember all You've spoken to us over the course of this study, and we ask for Your guidance and patience as we journey on from here. In Jesus's precious name we pray. Amen.*

# Notes


**Introduction**

1 The Cigna Group, "Loneliness in America 2025: A pervasive struggle requires a communal response," accessed July 22, 2025, https://newsroom.thecignagroup.com/loneliness-in-america.

**Week 1**

1 R. T. France, *The Gospel of Matthew* (Eerdmans, 2007), 91.

2 Andreas J. Köstenberger, *John*, BECNT (Baker Academic, 2004), 111.

3 Ben Witherington III, *Women in the Ministry of Jesus* (Cambridge University Press, 1984), 10-12; Craig S. Keener, *The IVP Bible Background Commentary: New Testament* (InterVarsity Press, 1993), 86.

4 Darrell L. Bock, *Luke 1:1–9:50*, Baker Exegetical Commentary on the New Testament (Baker Academic, 1994), 107-109.

5 Bock, *Luke 1:1–9:50*, 118; Andreas J. Köstenberger and Alexander E. Stewart, *The First Days of Jesus* (Crossway, 2015), 45.

6 N. T. Wright, *Luke for Everyone* (Westminster John Knox Press, 2004), 14-15.

7 Keener, *The IVP Bible Background Commentary: New Testament*, 52.

**Week 2**

1 Carl Toney, *Good News of God's Reign* (Abilene Christian University Press, 2025).

2 John Nolland, *Luke 1–9:20*, Word Biblical Commentary (Word Books, 1989), 27-28.

**Week 3**

1 Craig S. Keener, *A Commentary on the Gospel of Matthew* (Eerdmans, 1999), 91-92.

2 R. T. France, *The Gospel of Matthew* (Eerdmans, 2007), 53-54.

3 Wright, *Luke for Everyone*, 25-26.

4 Everett Ferguson, *Backgrounds of Early Christianity*, 3rd ed. (Eerdmans, 2003), 27-29.

5 N. T. Wright, *The New Testament and the People of God* (Fortress Press, 1992), 155-156.

6 John Bright, *A History of Israel*, 4th ed. (Westminster John Knox Press, 2000), 327-365.

7 Craig A. Evans, *Jesus and His World: The Archaeological Evidence* (Westminster John Knox Press, 2012), 29-31.

8 Joachim Jeremias, *Jerusalem in the Time of Jesus* (Fortress Press, 1969), 20-23.

9 F. F. Bruce, *Paul: Apostle of the Heart Set Free* (Eerdmans, 1977), 39-41.

10 Keener, *The IVP Bible Background Commentary*, 131-132.

11 France, *The Gospel of Matthew*, 50-51.

Week 4

1 Jeremias, *Jerusalem in the Time of Jesus*, 305-307.

2 Keener, *IVP Bible Background Commentary*, 132.

3 Nowadays, the command is translated much more narrowly as "You shall not murder" (Exodus 20:13).

4 Bock, *Luke 1:1–9:50*, 237-238.

5 Keener, *A Commentary on the Gospel of Matthew*, 93-94, 100-102.

6 Raymond E. Brown, *The Birth of the Messiah (Yale University Press)*, 187–189.

7 Paul L. Maier, *Herod the Grea*t (Kregel, 1998), 143-145.

8 France, *The Gospel of Matthew*, 87-88.

I want to meet you!
I would absolutely love to speak at your live gathering of 200 or more. Please feel free to reach out and invite me to your next event.
Lisa Torrey

# Also from Lisa Toney

**We are all flawed, but God can turn those weaknesses into strengths.**

The apostle Peter's passion and imperfections make him one of the Bible's most loved and relatable people. Even when Peter gave up, gave in, and gave out, Jesus was there for him. Join Lisa Toney as she follows Peter through his time with Jesus, from the beginning of Jesus's ministry to the Resurrection and through Pentecost, when Peter begins to live into his call. Along the way, discover the raw honesty of a man who veered from staunch devotion to moments of doubt, mirroring our own human struggles.

In the six-week Bible study *Perfectly Flawed*, we see that there is an unparalleled power Jesus gives that can only be found in our weakness. We discover the strength of Jesus that is available to each of us. Learn to persevere in your faith, live confidently, and boldly step into God's purpose for you. See how Peter's story is an invitation to embrace imperfection, find strength in the relentless grace of God, and discover how each one of us is perfectly flawed but still deeply loved by God.

Learn more at:
www.abingdonwomen.com
/bible-studies/perfectly-flawed

# Also from Lisa Toney

**Wait faithfully. Listen closely. March boldly.**

Ever feel like you're waiting forever for God to show up? You're not alone. Meet Deborah—a woman who knew something about divine timing that we desperately need to learn today.

Deborah wasn't just sitting around waiting for life to happen. She was a warrior, a wife, a prophet, and a judge who understood how to move in sync with God's perfect timing. Her story isn't just ancient history—it's a roadmap for anyone tired of rushing ahead or falling behind God's plan. In our instant-everything culture, Deborah's journey teaches us that the best things really do come to those who wait—and act when God says, "Go." Her warrior cry echoes through the ages: "March on with courage!"

Through this transformative journey with Deborah, you'll learn how to live with more patience and discover the power of perseverance. You'll spend more time enjoying God's presence while practicing listening for His voice. Most importantly, you'll remember that delays are not denials and learn to march on with courage in the midst of adversity.

Learn more at:
www.abingdonwomen.com
/bible-studies/not-one-moment-late